Beyond the Pixie Dust

Becoming an
Apprentice of the Kingdom

JOSH AVERY

Theme Park Press
The Happiest Books on Earth
www.ThemeParkPress.com

Editor: Bob McLain
Layout: Artisanal Text

ISBN 978-1-68390-305-5
Printed in the United States of America

Theme Park Press | www.ThemeParkPress.com
Address queries to bob@themeparkpress.com

CONTENTS

Introduction

My wife forced me to write this book.

Okay, so that's not entirely true...but although I've envisioned being an author since I was young, I certainly never once planned or desired to write a book in the genre of the one you're holding in your hands.

I'm not one to get misty-eyed while watching cheesy Christian movies that purport to be true stories. I'm not the kind of guy who picks up Disney related devotionals, eager to find some loose connection between Maleficent and the Devil. I have a book sitting on my shelf (given to me years ago by a fellow Pastor) that draws lines between Disney movies and Scripture passages...and I have yet to read even one chapter.

The truth is, I don't see great meaning in attempting to put 1st century Bible-verse-shaped puzzle pieces into the puzzle of 21st century theme park rides. Scripture wasn't meant to be like taffy at Goofy's Candy Company in Disney Springs, stretched out and manipulated until it fits the size and shape of which we'd like it to adhere.

Yet here I am, writing a book that involves matters of faith, trust, and yes—even pixie dust. If you're a skeptic like me, you're probably wondering what makes this book any different from all the others...or even more specifically, why I decided to change my mind in writing this.

Apart from my wife's continued insistence, what finally convinced me to sit down and type these words is that *Disney consistently reveals to me a Kingdom that is not found in Orlando, Anaheim, or any of its theme parks around the world.*

Why is it that so many of us can spend *years* attending church services and never be moved to a single tear, yet as soon as the anthem begins playing for the evening Happily Ever After fireworks show we find monsoons in our tear ducts?

Why do countless individuals spend their childhood dreaming of the moment they can grow up and become a Disney Cast Member? Why, for that matter, does simply walking down a road called Main Street, USA invoke such wonder and awe and amazement?

I wrote this book because, after all of my years attending and working in churches, I still find that the place I feel closest to the One who made me is in a Florida swampland that has been converted into a theme park.

That, of course, raises *all* sorts of questions.

And so I needed to write a book about it to sort through them. Thanks for joining me.

CHAPTER ONE

Storyboarding

Walt Disney is arguably the best storyteller who ever lived.

We can thank him directly for classic films like *Bambi, Cinderella, Peter Pan, Alice in Wonderland,* and *Pinocchio*—and that's only a beginning to the list of animated movies, to say nothing of the live action catalog he produced.

You may already know that the very first Disney animated movie was *Snow White and the Seven Dwarfs.* Released in 1937, Disney fans everywhere look to the adventures of Snow White as the catalyst to the film empire that we enjoy today. In retrospect, it's easy to forget just how much hinged on the success of this one girl and her seven small friends.

Pixar, the Marvel Cinematic Universe, Lucasfilm, Walt Disney World (to name just a few)...each and every one of them, likely to be totally different if Snow White would have bombed at the box office. The parks would probably not even exist.

What you may not be aware of is that Snow White was not only the first full length animated film created by the Disney company, it was *the* first full length animated film created. Ever. As in, no one had ever made anything longer than a cartoon short before this point.

Many people didn't believe that anyone would want to sit through an hour and a half of anything other than live action. It was going to take some convincing in order to get anyone on board, including his own team of animators.

But above all else, Walt believed in his story. He knew that if audiences could see the tale unfold on the big screen that had already unfolded within his mind, they would love it. He wasn't going to let the possibility of failure get in his way, and he moved forward with the first step of his plan one winter night in 1934.

Giving forty of his animators fifty cents each, Walt sent them all across the street from the Disney soundstage to get some dinner with instructions to return to meet him back on the property after they had all finished their meals. A short time later, the animators were back, curiously taking their seats in folding chairs Walt had arranged while they were eating.

In front of them was a single light bulb that acted as a spotlight, and one sole actor took the stage: Walt Disney himself. For the next hour, Walt singlehandedly played the part of every single character in the story of *Snow White and the Seven Dwarfs* by himself, using the creepy voice of the Witch when she appeared or deepening his voice for the role of the prince. His face took on a kind look when acting as Snow White, and resembled the stern and foreboding visage of the Evil Queen when necessary.

None of the forty animators were bored for a second, and all of their attention was kept through every single moment. When the amazing production eventually came to an end, Walt told them simply "That is going to be our first feature-length animated film."

No one argued and no one wondered how it would be done. In that moment, they knew without a doubt that it could be accomplished, because their leader, the legendary Walt Disney, had just unveiled the possibility before their very eyes.

Make no mistake, Walt knew the power of a good story. He not only believed making *Snow White* would bring a good return on their investment, thereby being a great financial decision—he certainly believed that the story would inspire and transform audiences across the world.

If people were willing to witness the story unfold, they would certainly be impacted.

Have you ever watched the movie about a couple who went to the store and picked out kitchen accessories? How about the full-length film about the boy who grows up to work in an office cubicle as an accountant? Remember the final scene, where he goes into the boss's office and gets a promotion?

I don't know about you, but *that* ending had me in tears the entire drive home.

Obviously, I'm being overly sarcastic. I wasn't crying at the end of that movie, because that movie doesn't exist. No one will ever go see a movie about a guy who works in an office cubicle or a film about that couple shopping at Bed, Bath, and Beyond. No wise production company would ever make that film, either, because it's obviously going to completely bomb at the box office.

When you begin to take an inventory of your favorite movies or stories, what you'll find is that *they all follow the exact same pattern*. Any story that hopes to inspire and transform an audience must follow this pattern, or it will likely fail.

Some might argue that not all stories follow this pattern, such as those in the horror genre. But again, we're only talking about movies that inspire or transform the viewer (for the better)...and horror doesn't fit that criteria.

The stories always begin with the main character living a relatively normal life—or a life of hardship. If he or she is perfect from the beginning, there's no room for improvement in their life and the story will have nowhere to go from here. They might be a bullied student, a faltering drug addict, or a homeless thief. Whoever the main character is, he or she is primed and ready for a change.

Shortly after the establishment of the lead character, every good story introduces what is known as the inciting incident. Depending on the tale, it may be an invitation from an old friend, the death of a loved one, or an impending apocalypse. Some incidents are chosen, while others are forced upon the individual. The inciting incident is the moment where something changes the course of their life forever...and once the character experiences it, they cannot go back to way things were beforehand.

Eventually, over the course of the bulk of the story, the character faces the problem the inciting incident has created and becomes a better off, stronger person than they were at the beginning. As the end credits roll, we feel a sense of comfort and accomplishment as we see them fully stepping into the new role that has come as a result of mastering their ordeal.

Think about it. Every story you know and love follows this pattern. Let's go back to *Snow White and the Seven Dwarfs*, and see if this holds true:

Snow White is a princess, but forced by her evil stepmother to work as a maid. She dreams of a better life, making a wish into a wishing well that her one true love will find her "today." She's ready for something new.

While in the forest, she learns from the Huntsman about the plot against her life, enacted by her evil stepmother, the Queen. This is the inciting incident, the moment that changes her life forever. After this scene, she will never be the same.

After meeting the dwarfs and facing the threat to her life as the Queen is defeated, Snow White accomplishes what she had hoped for in the beginning of the film. In the final scene, all the gathered dwarfs and animals cheer as the Prince brings Snow back to the castle for their happily ever after.

Normal existence.
Inciting incident.
Conflict.
Overcoming of the problem/defeat of evil.
Transformation is achieved and the new life begins.

We could take the time to make our way through all of the Disney company owned films and finds the same pattern emerging in vastly different stories:

A physically weak Steve Rogers undergoes an experimental program and becomes the powerful super soldier Captain America.

A devastated, lonely, and bitter old man named Carl Fredricksen is asked to move from his house and ends up finding a new family.

A farm boy who's biggest concern is "going into Toche Station to pick up some power converters" is eventually responsible for destroying the Death Star and defeating the evil Empire.

The list goes on and on, touching on all of the fictional stories that have inspired and transformed us over the years. That fact alone would be interesting, and there are people who have written at length about the details of story form and patterns we can find throughout.

But perhaps what I find even more interesting than the repeated pattern of the written story is the simple fact that, if we want to live an interesting and meaningful life, *we'll need to apply this same series of events to our life as well.*

What that means and how we can achieve it will be the main focus of the rest of this book, but for now it's important to begin with the realization that this pattern of

Normal existence.

Inciting incident.

Conflict.

Overcoming of the problem/defeat of evil.

Transformation is achieved and the new life begins.

reflects *the* Story, the story of humanity that is recorded throughout the bigger picture of Scripture.

You may have heard of storyboarding. This is a process that was actually invented by the Walt Disney Studios in the 1930s, and it's been used by countless companies and studios in film-making ever since. Essentially, it's a method of planning out the story by looking at the bigger picture, traditionally captured by a series of images put in sequential order on the wall.

Let's spend the rest of this chapter storyboarding the big picture of the Bible so we can see how it follows the same pattern as all of the other stories like *Snow White* and *Captain America*. This will be vital as we move forward for our understanding of where we personally fit into God's bigger picture and story, as well as how this all relates to our deep connection to the Disney stories and parks.

Obviously, we're not dealing with a medium where we can use images on the wall—so you'll need to create the images in your mind as we walk through them!

Did you ever get the feeling that things were never supposed to be as convoluted as the world we've found ourselves in? What was *meant* to be perfect, joyous living only lasts two short chapters at the beginning of Genesis. We don't know how long perfection lasted for Adam and Eve in reality—it could have been several days, a few weeks, or even decades.

What we do know is that by chapter three of Genesis, a "serpent" (who is much more than a simple snake) talks the happy couple into eating fruit from the tree which God has commanded them not to eat from. For humanity as a whole, this is the inciting incident, because from this point forward, everything has changed.

There's also echoes of the adventure ahead; a foreshadowing of what is to come and how this evil will finally be defeated. In Genesis 3:15, God tells this enemy: "he will crush your head, and you will strike his heel."

It's all a bit mysterious, and if we're picturing a literal green snake slithering around the garden of Eden, we might think that this message has something to do with a man in steel-toed boots smashing the head of a serpent that just scared his wife in the backyard. But in reality, this is already the beginning of the end for the adversary—we just have to wait to see how the story unfolds to figure out the riddle of his demise.

By Genesis 4, a brother has committed the first murder, slaughtering his own sibling in an act of jealously. It hasn't taken long for the story to derail, to move from the perfection and endless joy of walking daily with God to blood spilling on the ground.

The next chapters and following books in this literary collection called the Bible show us countless examples of the conflict we find ourselves in

from a nation of slaves in Exodus

to the retribution of Samson in Judges

to the evil domino-like choices of King David in 2 Samuel 11

to the destruction of the sacred temple in 2 Kings 25

to the near genocide that Esther must risk everything to prevent

to the total devastation of a man's entire life in the book of Job

to the Psalms that are filled with laments

to the revelation of priests who took advantage of people in Jeremiah 7

to the proclamation of judgment by Malachi

and the list goes on and on.

Each of these books in the Hebrew Scriptures (also called the "Old Testament" by some) are full of sub-stories; individual lives recorded over the course of thousands of years. We'll soon zoom in closer to this individual level, as our own stories that we're currently living can be found here—but for now, let's continue on the bird's eye view level, looking at the big picture story of Scripture.

All of this conflict reflected in the sub-stories of humanity leads us, of course, to some sort of solution. Only horror movies end with conflict and evil having the last word, and I am overjoyed to say that the story of humanity does not end with darkness triumphing.

In a series of four books that are different perspectives on the same series of events (Matthew, Mark, Luke, and John), we are introduced to the life and ministry of Jesus, a man who was revealed to be much more than a common Rabbi (the Jewish term for teacher). In Jesus, we are finally provided an answer to the riddle we received way back in Genesis 3.

Just when it seems like this Jesus might be the prom-ised Messiah (the one prophesied to restore Israel), he is killed on a Roman execution device called a cross as a common criminal. In many stories, the death of the hero seems to be the end of the tale—Sleeping Beauty falls into eternal slumber, Aslan is killed on the stone table, the Beast is stabbed by Gaston.

We might say that the serpent enemy has struck the heel of Jesus, injecting his venom with a deadly force.

But any avid fan of story knows that, in many of these tales, *death doesn't have the final word* for the hero. When it came to Jesus, three days after his seemingly final death revealed that not only was he alive...he had overcome death itself.

In a counter-intuitive twist in the story, the death and subsequent resurrection of Jesus is the very means by which he conquers death once and for all. Although he was dealt a blow from the serpent on the cross, he now completely crushes the head of the adversary in his resurrection.

Every moment after the resurrection is an invitation into the transformation and new life that is available through becoming an apprentice of Jesus. The books that follow those four Gospels still include conflict, but for followers of Jesus the conflict is no longer something that binds them.

Defining themselves as new creations, the first apprentices of Jesus like Paul and Barnabas and John face torture, famine, shipwreck, and even the threat of death from the Romans...and yet they unflinchingly continue to raise high the banner of love, grace, peace, and the Kingdom of God above the power of Rome.

To these first Christians, the new life wasn't something that everyone had to wait to achieve some day in a far off land called Heaven. According to them, this type of meaningful life, full of peace and joy, starts right now in the midst of the world's conflict.

Ultimately, a picture of hope and restoration is painted in a book called Revelation, but we're getting ahead of ourselves. Our storyboard of humanity is complete, giving us an idea of where we've been, how we got to where we are now, and a bit of the life available to us right here and right now.

But we all want to know specifically how we as individuals can enter into that meaningful kind of life ourselves. Many of us have attended church for years or prayed and read the Bible daily, yet still feel as if there's something lacking—like we've been living a boring story with our lives.

In order for us to address *that*, we'll need to head together to the *real* Seven Dwarfs Cottage, hidden away in the Florida woods about an hour and a half from the Magic Kingdom.

PART I

....

Normal Existence

CHAPTER TWO

Adventure in the Great Wide Somewhere

We already know a little bit from our time together about the early days of production on *Snow White and the Seven Dwarfs*...but it turns out that the most influential moment involving Snow White may not have been in 1934 at the Disney soundstage. I'm talking about the dwarfs cottage located in the state of Florida.

I know what you're thinking—you're probably picturing the one inside the Magic Kingdom, where guests can peek inside near the end of riding the popular Seven Dwarfs Mine Train coaster. But that cottage wasn't built until 2014 as a part of the New Fantasyland expansion, and I'm talking about a cottage that's existed since long before Walt Disney World ever broke ground.

The story is often told that Walt didn't come up with the idea for Disneyland until after his daughters were born. While he was sitting on a bench at an amusement park, eating peanuts and watching his daughters ride the carousel, he realized it would be great if there were a place that adults and kids could enjoy together. This tale is partly true, primarily because it is a story that we have handed down via recording by Walt Disney himself.

But while Walt may have traced back the origins of Disneyland to that park bench in retrospect, it's literally impossible for that story to be completely factual. I say this not to cast doubt on one of my favorite people of all time, but because Walt's original sketch of Disneyland is dated 1932, and his first daughter wasn't even born until 1933.

To give us an idea of the timeline here, Walt drew up rough plans for his park in 1932, he sat on the park bench with his peanuts sometime in the mid 1930s to early 1940s, *Snow White and the Seven Dwarfs* was released in 1937, and Disneyland opened the gates for the first day of operation in 1955. Walt launched the planning stages of what would become Walt Disney World in Florida in the early 1960s before his death.

But there's another event we should be aware of in the late 1930s, a monumental piece of history that attests to the amount of influence that the stories and characters Walt created have amongst the world.

In 1937, Judge Alfred Nippert faced what was undoubtedly the hardest year of his life. His beloved wife, Maud, had passed away, and in his grief Judge Alfred considered how he might positively use his free time. Maud's father, James Gamble, had passed on some property in Port Orange, Florida to the couple several years before.

Enter the premiere of *Snow White and the Seven Dwarfs*. Sadly, Alfred couldn't attend the showing with his wife, because she died shortly before it released in theaters. But remember what we learned in the last chapter—*Snow White* was revolutionary because it was the very first full length animated movie to ever exist. It impacted countless people who saw it, but Alfred took his love for the film to the next level.

His initial vision was to use the land from his father in law to build a small play house based upon the movie for his young nieces. That project alone would have been amazing; an automatic success amongst the little girls that would surely have elevated him to the status of "favorite Uncle." But as Alfred planned out the details, he knew he wouldn't be satisfied with a small playhouse version of his dream.

And that's how Judge Alfred Nippert ended up building a full scale model of the seven dwarfs cottage, a wishing well, the witch's hut, *and* a diamond mine right in the middle of the Port Orange property.

The cottage wasn't just an outward replica of the movie. Every detail inside was to be perfectly aligned with the imagination displayed by the animators in *Snow White*. Nippert required the carpenter who built it to watch the film several times, analyze frames printed from the movie, and attempt to re-create every detail as closely as possible in the real life construction.

The final product was an image straight from the screen into the real world. Walking inside, you would see a huge fireplace—and if you ventured up the stairs, you would find a bed with seven headboards inscribed with the names of all of the dwarfs.

Although it's hard to find much history written on the subject, it seems as if Walt himself visited the property in 1938 when the project was completed. There are no photos or videos documenting his visit, but the story looks to be correct. Shortly after his visit, Alfred received eight life size dolls in a delivery from the Walt Disney Company—seven dwarfs and one Snow White, all for use in making the cottage even more magical.

What's fascinating about this story is that since it seems clear Walt visited Judge Nippert's property, it makes this the very first time Walt would have experienced something he created with all of his five senses. In other words, up to this point all of his stories had been confined to storyboards, drawn pages, and film screens... but now, at Nippert's cottage, he experienced it firsthand.

For the first time, he was a part of the story.

We know that Walt dreamed of Disneyland as early as 1932, when he drew that sketch. But there are many who speculate, just like the inspiration while eating peanuts on the bench, that this simple moment of entering into the story stuck with him for years...and was a major influence in the creation of his park.

Some push the issue further, wondering if maybe Walt eventually looked into buying land in Florida because he resonated with the area during his visit with Alfred Nippert (and saw it as the perfect expansive place to make all of his future dreams become a reality). That is only speculation, but it's certainly interesting to consider nonetheless.

Regardless of the depth to which Walt was actually influenced by his visit to the cottage at Gamble Place, it seems inconceivable to imagine that he was not influenced at all. To some degree, being inside of his story had to have impacted him.

This is key to our understanding of our own stories and where we find ourselves in the bigger picture story that God is telling over time. Because as any avid film fan will tell you, going to the theatre and eating popcorn for the newest blockbuster only seems to fulfill our need for meaning until the credits begin rolling. At some point, it's not enough to just watch movies or read books about a character being invited into an adventure greater than themselves. There comes a time where we all realize that we want to experience that for ourselves.

If we're being honest with ourselves, we all resonate with Belle when she sings the words "I want adventure in the great wide somewhere. I want it more than I can tell."

Obviously, you're not be hoping to experience being locked in a Beast's castle, or reduced to a miniature size by your Dad's shrink ray, or abandoned by your parents on a desert planet named Jakku.

But we *do* want to experience something larger than ourselves; to know that we're a part of something meaningful that will transcend our nine to five jobs and weekly grocery shopping trips.

I think this is almost certainly the reason many dream about becoming Cast Members. It's one thing to spend your vacation on Walt Disney World property or to secure an annual pass. It's a completely different thing to *become* a part of the magic, to spend your working hours in the shadow of Cinderella Castle.

I'm also fairly certain that this is why so many people have attended church services for years, possibly even their entire life, and yet still feel so unfulfilled. It's all well and good to hear about people like David, Abraham, Peter, Esther, and the rest...but at the end of the day, we often see them as being a part of an amazing story while finding ourselves in a totally different category.

The people found upon the pages of Scripture were certainly more spiritual, higher-up-on-God's-totem-pole, better than we could ever ascribe or hope to be....right? I mean, these are what have been called the "heroes of the faith," and they were anything but normal. In fact, if there have ever been humans who we could compare to the heroes of the Marvel Cinematic Universe, it would be individuals like Samson, Moses, and Paul, wouldn't it?

We could never relate to heroes like that, because whether it's a guy who got bit by a radioactive spider or a man who led over 600,000 people out of slavery (Exodus 12:37), it's not possible to measure up. It certainly seems a far cry from "I'm April and I work as a dental hygienist." We read the stories of God, yet never can truly hope to be in one ourselves.

This is how many people have felt, yet taking a true look at the pages of Scripture reveals to us a different story. For whatever reason, we have only remembered the big moments of these people's lives—we've skipped the earlier parts and skipped right to the slaying of Goliath, the emerging from the den of lions, or the "saving of many lives" from a famine (1 Samuel 17, Daniel 6, and Genesis 50). We think that these people were unwavering in their faith and unbreakable in their zeal, and so they're not like us. But this isn't the full picture of reality.

Let's look at a specific example, found in 1 Kings 18:16-40. I encourage you to get a Bible and look it up before moving on, because that will give you the best understanding of the story we're talking about.

The odds are against Elijah as he solely takes on 450 prophets by himself. The challenge's details are clearly laid out: each side will build an altar and place the traditional bull upon the wood, but neither party will be allowed to light it with fire. To determine who serves the real god, each will get the chance to pray or do whatever they feel necessary in order to get the attention of their god, who will then respond with lighting the fire supernaturally.

Elijah is already the underdog, but then he decides to take it to the next level. He will give the 450 prophets of Baal the first pick of the sacrifice (the bull), and he'll let them have a turn all to themselves before he begins praying to his God.

All day long, these 450 men make fools of themselves as they verbally shout, dance around the altar, and even begin cutting their own flesh with their swords and spears, pouring their own blood on the altar. All of this in the hopes that their crazy antics might get the attention of their god Baal, who would then ignite the flame that would announce them as the winners.

Elijah even gets into the fun, sarcastically calling out things like "You need to be louder, he's probably sleeping!" or "Maybe he's on the toilet!"

Eventually, the silence of Baal has gone on for so long that it's embarrassing for them to go on any longer, and Elijah finally gets his turn as evening arrives. At this point in the narrative, we might assume that he would get right to work, saying a prayer for his God to light the fire on his sacrifice...but he wants to make things a little more complicated first.

Getting the help of the gathered crowd, he fills up four large jars with water and pours them all over the sacrifice. It drips down the bull and the wood. He asks them to do it a second time, eight large jars now having been spilled on the altar. It's starting to get pretty soggy. Just when the people are questioning if Elijah knows that water *isn't* a fire starter, he tells them to get 4 more large jars to pour.

Those of us who passed first grade math can affirm that's now twelve full jars. There has been so much water poured over the entire thing that now it's filling up a trench that Elijah had dug around the altar like a moat.

And then comes Elijah's prayer. It stands in stark contrast to the frenetic performance of the prophets of Baal that took all day long; it's recorded within two verses and probably took a total of thirty seconds to speak.

Immediately following the simple prayer, Elijah's altar ignites with not only fire to burn up the sacrifice—it's a fire so hot that it consumes the wood, the stones, burns the dirt underneath, and even dries up the water in the makeshift moat.

Pretty big success for a single guy facing 450 enemies. The victory here seems effortless, which of course it was, given that the one true God was involved. It reminds me of Thor wielding Mjölnir, destroying the enemy with his hammer singlehandedly (even though Elijah's battle didn't involve a weapon).

This is one of those larger than life stories that cause us to elevate people like Elijah to an unattainable level of reality. But in the middle of these types of thoughts, sitting amazed at the victory of 1 Kings 18, we end up overlooking what happens in the very next chapter, in 1 Kings 19:1-5.

Immediately following the success of Elijah we just read about, the evil Queen (there's *always* an evil Queen in good stories, isn't there?) gets wind of how not only had her prophets failed at the challenge, but all 450 had been killed by Elijah and the crowd.

Obviously, she wasn't happy about this outcome. She sends out a threat via her messenger, swearing by her gods that within twenty four hours she will end Elijah's life just like he killed her men.

We would think that Elijah would feel pretty confident at this point. Sure, the evil Queen Jezebel is trying to kill him by all means necessary. Yes, she's just released a demented message that gives him one more day to live. But given that Elijah *literally* just experienced God overcoming 450 of his enemies with nothing other than a half minute prayer and twelve counter-intuitive jars of water to light a fire...he shouldn't have anything to worry about.

Except a confident, shoulders-held-high, emotionally strong prophet of God isn't the picture we get when the story returns to our friend Elijah. Not only is Elijah afraid of the Queen's edict, he's *suicidal*.

You didn't read that wrong. When he hears the news, he runs out by himself into the desert and prays that he might die, asking God to take his life before laying down under a tree in desperation. Remember that this takes place in the ancient world, in a specific culture that strongly believed that physically taking your own life was *never* an option, regardless of how bad things had gotten. The ancient Israelites had a deeply held conviction that since God created human life, only He could permit the ending of a life.

In other words, the closest thing permissible to killing yourself in the ancient Jewish world was praying that the God who created your life would take it away. And that's exactly where we find Elijah after his infamous victory.

So wait...Elijah struggled with depression? He dealt with the lowest of low thoughts after a huge emotional and spiritual high? He's not an invincible superhero who is unaffected by the realities of the real world? He's a real person who seemed to feel anxiety and uncertainty and darkness, and his story is recorded in the Scripture?

Yep.

Does that remind you of anyone? Primarily...yourself? I mean, I've never been diagnosed with clinical depression, nor can I claim to know what it's like to struggle with the kind of depression I have seen many close to me fight over the course of their lives.

But I've *definitely* spent more than a few days of my life wondering how one day could be so completely amazing, followed by a day where nothing seems right in the world. At times, there's not even a traceable reason I have those dark feelings—it's just a deep sadness, where everything has the flavor of negativity.

When I really take a look into the bigger picture story that God is telling through the pages of Scripture, what's interesting to find is that it's ultimately about ordinary people joining into the adventure. Or to put it another way, it's about those who have absolutely nothing special or significant about them becoming significant, *not* because of their own merit or importance but because God has brought meaning into their story.

Noah faced an embarrassing situation after getting drunk and falling asleep naked in his tent (Genesis 12:11-20). Abraham lied twice to two different Kings about his wife because he was scared (Genesis 20:1-17). David was involved in an affair and tried to cover it up (2 Samuel 11). Solomon put his faith in riches, Egypt, and women (1 Kings 10:14-11:13).

Do we really need to continue through the other books in the Bible's collection?

The point of these stories has, at times, been misconstrued. They aren't recorded to show that it's okay to commit the same sins as these people, and they don't prove the Bible is full of fake and hypocritical tales.

The stories reflect the reality of the average human life, ordinary people who even make big mistakes—yet are still chosen by God to join into the amazing narrative that He's telling in the world. Wouldn't it be depressing if it was the other way around, if the pages of Scripture only talked about people who had never made mistakes in their lives?

Firstly, that would be unbelievable, because it's *not possible*. And secondly, it would be unattainable to the rest of us who would be lower on the totem pole, unable to measure up.

The good news is that we, like the people who fill the 66 books of the Bible, actually *can* enter into the story. So if you're April the dental hygienist, Jeremy the accountant, or Derek the plumber...you can be assured that God is inviting you into the adventure in the great wide somewhere.

The bad news (at least on the surface) is that you're not going to be successful without a guide who will come alongside you.

CHAPTER THREE

Correction— I Know Your Father

For any story to be compelling, the main character needs to be in a space where change and growth is necessary. In other words, they can't be perfect and have it all together in the opening scene.

If he or she is practically perfect in every way, then there's no need for the transformation that comes with the ensuing adventure. And if there's no adventure, you'll have a boring story. Even in the case of rich, famous, and popular characters like the know-it-all Tony Stark must realize throughout his story arc that he doesn't have it all figured out...he needs to grow as an individual.

In fact, Mary Poppins is often described as perfect in every way, but I would argue that she's not the main character in the film that shares her name, thus why it isn't a boring story. It seems to me that the person who experiences the full range of transformation (and thus is the main character) in *Mary Poppins* is actually the father, George Banks...but maybe that deep dive is another book entirely.

We've already established the normal existence phase of the character, but what we need to understand now is the need (in many stories) for a Guide to come along-side the hero. The Guide often knows much more than the hesitant adventurer about what's to come, how they might be successful, and even about some dangers they might face along the way.

Some of the most cherished Guides in our favorite stories include Grandmother Willow, Mrs. Potts, the Fairy Godmother, Yoda, Hector, Mushu, Baloo, Genie, Jiminy Cricket, and more. Each of these Guides give key, important advice and guidance to the heroes and heroines in order to help lead them to the next step in their journey. Without a Guide, the character can quickly get off task, move off course, or get derailed from the mission they've been given.

Continuing with that conversation we started a moment ago, it seems clear to me that Mary Poppins is, in fact, the Guide in her own movie. She guides George Banks through the transformation that he needs to fly a kite with the children within the final scenes.

The Divine Guide

Of course, the ultimate Guide throughout the ongoing story of history (and therefore our own adventures) is God Himself. We seek after His guidance and His wisdom in order to determine where to go and what to do next in our lives. While this is a well known fact of the Christian life, it can become "Christianese" pretty quick.

In other words, while everyone talks about the importance of hearing the voice of God and following His leading for our lives, most of us struggle to know how we can actually accomplish it. That feeling of being powerless to hear His voice results in many people giving up on seeking it entirely.

In truth, God wants to speak to us—and two of the ways He speaks are far from rocket science. To the contrary, they are easily accessible methods of hearing, discerning, and following God's voice.

The first way we hear God's voice is through His Word, meaning the 66 books of the Bible. That may seem like the cheesy Sunday School answer, but it's true. Remember that in Scripture, we read about the stories of people who lived in our world and how they dealt with the same kinds of struggles that we deal with on this same planet today. Although societies, nations, and all sorts of things change over the years, God Himself never changes or becomes different.

God's unchangeability is made clear time and time again throughout the Scriptures: Hebrews 13:8, Malachi 3:6, James 1:17, Psalm 102:27, and countless others. Additionally, the implications of God calling Himself "I AM" in Exodus 3 and elsewhere infer that He is always the same. These continued promises provide a clear window into the truth that we can truly rest in His Word to us as never changing day to day or moment to moment, as many other things around us will.

Of course, we also see in Scripture (specifically in the four Gospels) the person and life of Jesus. The stories and teachings of Jesus give us a unique look into the calling God has for us as His apprentices, because Jesus was 100 percent human while still remaining 100 percent God. His life gives us the perspective we often need to know what to do next.

While grasping the idea of God and His will for us can sometimes seem hard to wrap our minds around, learning from the human person of Jesus is not only possible to replicate—doing what Jesus did and becoming like Him is what we should be striving to accomplish.

Beyond the Scripture, we can also hear God's voice as a Guide when he speaks His thoughts and will directly into our minds. As I write that, I know that the sentence I've just typed can end up being taken in very dangerous way, so it needs to be unpacked and explained.

Check out Isaiah 55:8-9:

> "For my thoughts are not your thoughts, neither are your ways my ways," declares the LORD. "As the heavens are higher than the earth, so are my ways higher than your ways and my thoughts higher than your thoughts."

That seems pretty straightforward. This verse has been quoted many times over countless years and by tons of people, and the majority of the time we've used it to explain that we can never hope to understand what God is thinking, simply because He's so high above us and His thoughts are unreachable. If that's true, then (besides the words of Scripture) we're limited on how God can speak to us as a Guide in our adventure.

If we're willing to check out the other verses in that same chapter, though, we'll quickly find that the theology behind the statement that "God's thoughts are unknowable" is actually false. Start right in verse one of chapter 55:

> Come, all you who are thirsty, come to the waters; and you who have no money, come, buy and eat! Come, buy wine and milk without money and without cost. Why spend money on what is not bread, and your labor on what does not satisfy?

So here, right at the beginning, we get an invitation from God to "buy and eat." Of course, He's talking about metaphorical food and drink, but that doesn't make things less confusing. How are we supposed to join the invitation to buy the supplies we need if we "have no money" as the verse indicates?

It's simple. From the very beginning of this passage, God is inviting people to receive what they need the most freely through Him. In other words, He's giving it away, and His free gift won't cost us anything.

And this free gift isn't just some lousy giveaway, like those tarnished "gold" charms you can pick up for free at the jewelry stores after disembarking at Disney Cruise Line ports. Verse 2 defines the symbolic food as "the richest of fare." This is the best of the best stuff that God is offering here.

But if the gift He's offering is so great and fantastic, then what is it beyond the symbolism and the metaphor? If there's something God is freely giving away, then I definitely want a part of it.

Our first clue is found in the greater context of Scripture. In the Bible, bread is repeatedly connected to the spoken word of God. A few examples:

> Man does not live by bread alone, but by every word that proceeds from the mouth of God.
>
> —Deuteronomy 8:3

And then there's Jeremiah, who takes the word/bread metaphor to the next level by talking about chowing down on words:

> When your words came, I ate them; they were my joy and my hearts delight.
>
> —Jeremiah 15:16

So the bread here that is being offered as a free gift in Isaiah 55 are the words of God. And this is exactly what we're seeking in our lives—a message and direction from God that will guide us further down the path He has planned for us.

We can freely receive His words without any cost to ourselves, but we will need to give up something in exchange. This much is clear in verse 7:

> Let the wicked forsake his way and the evil man his thoughts.

Our own ideas about how things should work out so often get in the way, don't they? If we're honest with ourselves, we'll see our own thoughts often impede our progress towards living a better story with our lives. If we want to clearly hear God's input regarding our journey, we'll need to turn away from the muddying sound of our own voice. (We'll talk more about this later in chapter 4.)

And that's where the famous verse 8 comes in: to point out that yes, God's thoughts are not our thoughts and His ways are not our ways—so we'll need to replace our ways with His.

Isaiah 55 has never been about trying to convince us that we'll never be able to understand God's thoughts for our life. In reality, *it's completely the opposite*. God wants to send His thoughts and His ways down from Heaven to Earth, which is the point Isaiah makes in verses 9 and 10.

God wants to tell you His plan for your life; He wants to tell you the next step in your journey. He wants to be the primary Guide in your story, and without hearing His thoughts and following His voice, your journey is essentially doomed to fail. (If you're interested in seeing more proof on this theology, start by checking out 1 Corinthians 2:9-16, Romans 8:6 & 26, Matthew 10:19-20, and James 1:5.)

But we must keep a key warning in mind as we discern God's call on our lives: any word God speaks to you will never contradict Scripture. Remember, as we've already established, He never changes—so you won't hear some brand new message that is completely unlike the One we read about in the Bible. You're not going to receive advice from God that makes excuses for sin or down a path that is contrary to His written word.

Let God's Holy Spirit be your Guide.

The Human Guide

It's easy to let that be the end of the discussion, to talk about how God guides our lives and then move on to planning the details of the journey itself. But the truth is, our adventure is even more likely to succeed if we establish another human person in our lives who can provide wisdom and guidance during our lifelong explorations.

Growing up in youth group, we used to call this person an accountability partner. In theory, it was supposed to be a friend in your life who you trusted to talk with struggles about. But in reality, an accountability partner in those days was often someone you *did* hang out with... but rarely (if ever) talked about serious issues with.

If your youth pastor asked, you could proudly proclaim "My accountability partner is Kevin!," when it didn't amount to much more than playing Nintendo 64 during overnighters.

If we truly want to succeed in making our life story meaningful, we'll need to find at least one human Guide who can play the ongoing role of Rafiki in our lives. I'm guessing that's not where you expected me to go with this, but stick with me...

The Lion King is a classic and fantastic example of the human Guide, although ironically it's a story featuring only animals and no people at all. The symbolism is there, though, and we're smart to consider what role the wise monkey plays in the tale.

Think about where we find Simba in the second half of the film. He's supposedly embraced a "hakuna matata," no-worries-lifestyle, but in reality he is haunted by the death of his father, on the run from his past, and avoiding the steps he needs to take to address the problems which now plague the pride in the form of Scar.

Even a visit from his best friend (and now, new girl-friend) Nala doesn't convince him to return and face the rest of his story. It's not until Simba runs off to be alone that he encounters the old baboon who forces him to dive back into the conflict.

Despite all of the years Simba has spent trying to hide away and distance himself from his previous identity, Rafiki knows who he truly is—and he knows how to invoke Simba's curiosity.

"I'm not the one who's confused. You don't even know who you are," Rafiki offers.

Simba responds sarcastically, "Oh, and I suppose you know?"

Rafiki doesn't give a long, detailed response. Mysteriously and cryptically, he simply says "Sure do; you're Mufasa's boy! Bye!" before running off away from Simba.

When Simba finally catches up to him, Rafiki reveals that he has not only lost track of his true identity, but he has also failed to realize that his father, Mufasa, is more alive than he knew.

All of this leads to one of the most famous scenes in the film, where Rafiki leads Simba to the water's edge. Eventually, Mufasa appears and speaks to his son from the heavens. Mufasa reminds Simba of his true identity as the King, and encourages him to return back into the narrative of his life, to engage in the conflict that will lead to freedom for the pride and a greater life for all.

If we want to take something spiritual from this story and strip away some of the metaphor, we could say that we're like Simba, often forgetting our identity in Christ and getting lost along the way on the epic adventure God has for us. We like to claim that we are living the hakuna matata good life because we have a nice job and a new flat screen, but if we're honest with ourselves all of the pain and the purposelessness hides just under the surface.

The symbolism would reveal Mufasa character as being like God, who reminds us of our true identity in Him when we listen to the lies around us that get us off track from the story He's invited us into.

But we also all need a person in our lives like Rafiki. He wasn't the one to deliver the message about Simba's identity, but he was a major contributor in pointing the way to the one who could. In our lives, if we hope to succeed we'll need to invite the advice and guidance of another person who will help us stay on track in the story we're living.

The founder of the Methodist tradition, John Wesley, believed strongly in this idea. He created what is called the band meeting, a small group of 2 to 5 people who meet weekly in order to keep each other on task in the adventure God is leading them through. To avoid the awkwardness of not knowing what to say (like in the old youth group accountability meetings), Wesley came up with a series of five questions that could guide such a gathering:

1. How is your soul? (In other words, how are you *really* doing on a deep and spiritual level?)

2. What are your struggles and successes since our last meeting?

3. How might the Spirit and Scriptures be speaking in your life?

These first three questions are easier to answer for most people. As you can imagine, if you know you're going to be answering a question like "how is the Scripture speaking in your life," you're much more likely to spend some time that week reading the Bible. This is the accountability aspect we talked about.

Once you're comfortable with the other member(s) of your band, you can move onto the two final, deeper questions:

4. Do you have any sin that you want to confess?

5. Are there any secrets or hidden things you would like to share?

Questions like this take a large amount of trust and vulnerability, but the end result is a clearer vision for your life and a stronger relationship with God and others. No one is able to successfully navigate the adventure alone, because as humans we consistently forget who we are and stumble around in the darkness of uncertainty as a result.

Whether you decide to form a band meeting, consult on a consistent basis with a mentor, or sign up for counseling to help deal with the trauma of your past to confront and conquer your future like Simba, identifying who your Guide is will be absolutely vital to the next steps in your journey.

Often, these Guides will dare us to take a step, an uncomfortable move in the direction of living a more meaningful story with your life. All of that, of course, leads us to a discussion about devouring an enormous ice cream sundae on Main Street, U.S.A....

PART II

Inciting Incident

CHAPTER FOUR

I Dare to Take Risks

I've lost count trying to keep track of the times I've visited Walt Disney World. I think my first visit was in 1996 (when I was ten) and I'm certain that my most recent visit was in early 2020 (before the pandemic hit). But beyond that, I've been on property so many times that it would be impossible to remember them all.

I don't take this for granted. I know that many families spend their entire lives dreaming of, planning for, and saving money for *one* trip—and here I am unable to even count mine.

What I've noticed as a return guest is that over the years the magic hasn't faded for me, it's just *transformed*. In my younger years, my main concern was riding all of my favorite attractions as quickly as possible, dragging my parents and siblings along at a hurried pace. I didn't want to get to the end of the vacation and realize I'd missed anything.

Now that I'm older, I find more enjoyment in the magic of the details: from all of the hidden background touches that Imagineers put into the buildings to the storylines that subtly guide the areas you're walking through. In short, the magic now comes to me not by rushing from one attraction to the next, but instead by slowing down and taking each moment for what it's worth.

When you're no longer necessarily concerned with hitting all the major attractions in a park within a day, you can come up with all sorts of new goals, challenges, or dares to complete. Annual pass holders, I know you're tracking with me on this...

Several years ago, my wife and I managed to visit all four parks at Walt Disney World in a day, eating and riding something at each. Extra time at EPCOT on a recent trip allowed me to discover some of the hidden treasures in World Showcase. A desire to see more of Magic Kingdom than normally experienced led me to take two behind the scenes tours, "Keys to the Kingdom" and "Marceline to Magic Kingdom."

There are all sorts of blogs, books, and even tweets that have been created by veteran guests, offering up varied ideas like these ones to deepen and expand the enjoyment of return trips. Some ideas seem like really grasping at straws (such as riding Spaceship Earth six times in a row to select all the different languages available) while many are fun challenges (like trying to become an extra at Indiana Jones).

In my opinion, though, the best kind of challenges are the ones that involve food. We all know that there's really no bad choice when it comes to selecting a meal or snack on Disney property. Everything is great, World Showcase is literally an entire smorgasbord of global culinary culture, and some of the often overlooked restaurants hide menu items that (once discovered) will keep you returning every trip.

This is where the giant ice cream sundae comes in. If you thought I had forgotten about it from the last chapter, you're mistaken—because once you see it, it's impossible to forget. Available at the Main Street Ice Cream Parlor for $22.99, the Mickey Kitchen Sink Sundae comes served in, you guessed it, a plastic mickey themed kitchen sink.

Inside of that sink you'll find three large scoops of chocolate, vanilla, and strawberry ice cream, all topped with hot fudge, caramel, strawberry sauce, chocolate chips, peanut butter chips, whipped cream, and (of course) three cherries on top.

I know there's many of you reading over that list of ingredients, dripping saliva on this book right now and saying to yourself or your loved ones: "I could definitely eat that whole thing by myself."

And who knows, maybe you could summon up your inner Winnie-the-Pooh and devour it with a rumbly in your tumbly. Certainly you'll have a rumbly in your tumbly when you're finished, to say the least. Look out City Hall restrooms.

But don't be deceived. Many have approached the sundae with high expectations and good intentions, only to realize later on why it's marked as a serving size for four people. The sink might not seem very wide, but it's pretty deep—and that's what will trip you up if you take on the challenge to attempt eating it by yourself.

These are the types of challenges that returning guests discover and dare each other to preform that a one time pass-through of the parks might not reveal. Walt Disney World is all about making the memories of a lifetime, and there are endless ways to achieve that.

But at the end of the day, I'm less interested in exactly *what* those memories involve and far more interested in *why* we're so eager to repeat them. Many of us dream about, plan, and return to the parks to make those additional memories because we find meaning in those moments. And, as we've already talked about, I would argue that we find deep meaning in those moments because we want to place ourselves into a story greater than ourselves.

The problem is, most of the epic challenges we've designed for ourselves turn out to be short lived. As amazing as it would be to tell your friends on Instagram that you finished the Mickey Kitchen Sink Sundae with before and after pictures, the excitement is going to be really short-lived.

After a couple of days of comments and likes, you're right back at square one, looking for another moment of meaning. Sure, it was fun finally getting to be "that guy" in the Monsters Inc. Laugh Floor show, but a few moments later, you're standing back out in the hot Florida sun with nothing to show for it except a sticker that proclaims "*I was that guy at Monsters Inc. Laugh Floor.*"

Yep. You were. It happened. Anyone want to cool off by riding Carousel of Progress?

Our problem as humans isn't necessarily that we've never identified our desire of wanting to be a part of something meaningful. The problem is that we can't figure out how to obtain it, and we have trouble discerning what that meaningful adventure might be.

There are times that we are reminded of how short life truly is, even if we end up living for 80-90 years. When it's all said and done, the reality is that things move quickly—and we feel as if we're seeing our kids in diapers one day and the next they're raising their own.

The more we are reminded of this truth, the more urgent finding meaning becomes, because none of us want to get to the end of our lives and have missed purpose. The question moves from "why am I searching for meaning?" to "what is meaning?," and it's possibly the most important question to which we could find an answer.

If you ask 20 different people what they think is most important in life and what can bring true purpose, you'll probably get 20 different answers. This is likely because, as humans, we are constantly trying all sorts of various things in an effort to find adventure in the great wide somewhere.

For some, it's work projects. For others, the answer might involve family. For yet another, you might hear something about a social activism cause that they're involved with. The list goes on and on, and it seems hard to really figure out if all of these answers are valid, or if maybe there could be something a little more concise.

All of this reminds me of a book in the Hebrew Scriptures called Ecclesiastes. At a surface level glance, it's really quite a depressing book. The author, who most believe was the King Solomon, writes about all of his pursuits of pleasure and meaning during this life, and they all turn out to be worthless.

According to his reflections, he tried tons of different strategies in order to find something worthwhile: studying and learning, gardening, relationships, getting more money, and more. (The corresponding verses are these, in order of those mentioned: Ecclesiastes 1:13, 2:4-5, 2:8, and 5:10.)

All we need to do is glance at the chapter headings to get an idea of what Solomon's final decision was regarding all of these ventures: "Wisdom is meaningless, pleasures are meaningless, toil is meaningless, advancement is meaningless." When we look into the text of the 12 chapters of Ecclesiastes, we find even more examples. If we had to summarize his thoughts on the purpose of life, we could basically just say...wait for it...

everything is meaningless.

Even when Solomon seems to start out with some good advice in chapter 9, he ends up going right back to his same old rhetoric:

> Enjoy life with your wife, whom you love, all the days of this meaningless life that God has given you under the sun—all your meaningless days. For this is your lot in life and in your toilsome labor under the sun.
>
> —Ecclesiastes 9:9

He started out so positive, and then just in case we didn't remember his gloomy outlook, he ends up repeating himself and then essentially says "well, that's all your life is going to amount to, so enjoy it while you can."

Better book that stay at the Grand Floridian with dinner at Victoria and Albert's (the most expensive hotel/restaurant combo on Walt Disney World property) while you still have the chance, because pretty soon you'll be dead and buried. Oh, and have a magical day!

In all seriousness, some of the content in Ecclesiastes seems like something I might expect to read in a book written by an atheist who believes that this life is all there is and there is no greater purpose to the universe. Of all places, I wouldn't think that I would find a message about meaninglessness in life in the Bible.

But what if Solomon, in all of his wisdom, was actually imparting a hidden truth to us that we would do well to understand and actualize in our lives? What if he had figured out something in the midst of his endless meaningless search that would allow us to find something that actually *did* matter?

Even though Solomon continued on for 11 chapters regarding how insignificant many pursuits end up being, he ends up in the final 14 verses of the book discussing what really matters. It may sound like the standard "church answer," but he ends up declaring that the most important thing we could possibly do would be to focus ourselves on God. He gives a few metaphors for our impending death and the urgency of this focus:

> Remember him—before the silver cord is severed, or the golden bowl is broken; before the pitcher is shattered at the spring, or the wheel broken at the well, and the dust returns to the ground it came from, and the spirit returns to God who gave it.
> —Ecclesiastes 12:6-7

> Now all has been heard; here is the conclusion of the matter: Fear God and keep his commandments, for this is the whole duty of man. For God will bring every deed into judgment, including every hidden thing, whether it is good or evil.
> —Ecclesiastes 12:13-14

So again, Solomon claims that before we die, our best bet towards living meaningfully would be to keep the commandments of God. Okay. That sounds like a completely spiritual, well-meaning, religious bottom line. We're now hearing something that I would expect to find in the pages of the Bible.

But I'm still not sure that it provides me with the kind of specific guidance that I'm looking for. If we want to live purposefully the kinds of stories that will rival the greatest stories of all time, then we need a specific direction.

Have you ever watched a movie that had too many plot lines or characters? Those are the worst, because the narrative is too confusing to follow. You think that you're watching a movie about a bank robbery, when the scene shifts and you find yourself viewing a couple of spies in the Swiss Alps. Right as the action culminates on the mountain, the perspective changes yet again and there's a guy sitting on his couch in sweatpants watching a football game.

Now you've been introduced to at least 5 characters in totally different settings in the span of three scenes, and you have *no idea* what in the world this movie is supposed to be about. Because there are so many simultaneous plot lines, not even one of them can be clear. Ultimately, there's no defined purpose.

I can't think of one Disney or Pixar movie that makes this fatal error. It's because the Walt Disney Company have spent decades studying, learning, and producing stories that have memorable characters, exciting adventures, and clear goals for their protagonists that must be achieved in order for good to prevail.

I wish that it was this easy for us in everyday life, but we tend to make it more difficult than it needs to be. At times, we keep piling on roles to the point that none of them can be clearly defined anymore. Some of us aren't living meaningfully because we are stretched thin between 250 different plot lines in life, and every single one of them suffer as a result.

When it comes to Solomon's bottom line here, it feels almost too broad. It's one thing to say we should follow the commandments of God and then everything will start to make sense in our lives...but it's another when we begin to look at what that might look like.

To be precise, the Jewish tradition reports that there are 613 commandments written in the Torah, which is the law written down by Moses in Genesis through Deuteronomy. So to clarify the conclusion of Ecclesiastes in light of this new information, we should focus ourselves on obeying 613 different laws if we're hoping to discover the one thing in life that isn't as meaningless as chasing after the wind.

I don't know about you, but I'm not able to focus on 5 different things, let alone 613. Is there some easier way to consolidate this list or a method of understanding the world that could lead me towards this greater way of living?

It turns out that there's a *much* easier way of thinking about how we follow these commands, and we have Jesus to thank for providing it to us. In Matthew 22:37-40, Jesus tells us two quick and easy phrases that summarize all 613 of those laws:

> "Love the Lord your God with all your heart and with all your soul and with all your mind." This is the first and greatest commandment.
>
> And the second is like it: "Love your neighbor as yourself." All the Law and the Prophets hang on these two commandments.

While this statement from Jesus is deeply profound, it's also amazingly simple. We don't need to worry about memorizing that huge list of laws, because if you truly love God with all your heart, mind, and soul, you probably won't make idols or desecrate holy things. And likewise, if you love your neighbor, you won't end up defrauding them or mistreating them. (All of these examples of laws are found in Leviticus 19, verses 4, 8, 13, and 33.)

What matters in this life? Anything that falls under the category of loving God or loving other people. Everything else might be amusing or a fun way to spend an afternoon, but at the end of the day, it's all ultimately meaningless.

All of this leads us back to where we started in this chapter, because we've all felt that rush of adrenaline that comes with these fleeting moments, and we all know how they aren't going to fulfill us.

The strange thing is that while we could all agree upon Jesus' assessment, focusing on living out stories that involve loving God or neighbor are often set on the back burner of our lives.

I could get to know my neighbor better by inviting them over to my house for dinner, or I could pick the much less awkward choice of spending my evening watching *The Mandalorian* by myself on Disney+. Most of the time, it's easy to get over any potential guilt about not choosing the meal. I'll get to the invite another day, right?

But if we're honest...after a session of binge watching, all I have to show for my invested time is having completed an amazing season of television. And the truth is, there's truly no meaning in any of it, regardless of what we tell ourselves. If there is a sliver, it's nothing compared to what we would have experienced if we would have chosen the meal.

As humans, we seem to be wired to choose the path of least resistance. In other words, unless we have a pretty good reason to choose the hard path, we'll just go with whatever's easiest and make excuses for ourselves—and these easy paths lead us to living more and more of the boring stories we hope to avoid.

It's almost as if Jesus knew what He was talking about when He said that we should

> Enter through the narrow gate. For wide is the gate and broad is the road that leads to destruction, and many enter through it. But small is the gate and narrow the road that leads to life, and only a few find it.
>
> —Matthew 7:13-14

Unless we're essentially forced to, many of us will never take the important step of moving towards the things that actually matter on that narrow path, the "whole duty" of loving God and loving our neighbor.

That leads us to a key piece of every single great story that has ever been written: the inciting incident. You might remember that the inciting incident is the event during which the main character moves from a normal existence into the adventure that will transform them forever.

If we want to achieve a tremendous goal of adventure in our lives, we'll probably need to introduce some sort of inciting incident to force ourselves out the door and into the story. This almost always involves a level of risk on our part. Walt Disney employed this strategy often:

"I dream, I test my dreams against my beliefs, *I dare to take risks*, and I execute my vision to make those dreams come true."

The dare to take a risk comes with an element of knowing that there is a possibility of failure. At the end of 2015, I decided that I wanted to run the full Walt Disney World Marathon to raise money for the Rescue Mission of the Mahoning Valley, the homeless shelter in my local area.

I've never considered myself a runner. In high school, I was on the track team at my small school, but only because all of my friends were on the team. I was almost always in last place in all of the races, and one time I even hid in the bathroom at a track meet to avoid running the 2 mile when my coach tried to rope me into it at the last minute.

I got into running 5k distances (3.1 miles) here and there in adulthood, but I always shook my head at people I knew who ran marathons. When I had the idea to raise money for the Rescue Mission, I knew I could get more funds if I ran a larger distance...but going from running 3 miles to 26 was not something I really wanted to do deep down.

As much as I love traveling around Disney property, I would rather take the air-conditioned buses than travel to each park *and* the entirety of ESPN Wide World of Sports by foot in a span of 6 hours. They don't call it the "wide" world by mistake. I felt like I was running around in there for years.

I can tell you from experience that there's a level of

being exhausted from walking around all day at a crowded Magic Kingdom that is absolutely nothing compared to traveling the entire property in the span of one morning.

The journey was not something I wanted to partake in, but the end result *was* something I desired. I loved the idea of both crossing the finish line and having raised as much money as possible for the shelter at the same time. In other words, what I liked was the idea of the accomplishment, of the final product, of the climactic scene.

I just didn't like the conflict I knew it would take to get to that point, the muscle cramps and dripping sweat that would accompany me on the journey—not to mention the months of training, including running in Ohio's winter temperatures. I needed something to force me into that conflict so that I could achieve the climactic scene.

In order to get myself through the process and struggle I would face on the way to achieving my goal, I needed to find a way to force myself into the commitment. It turned out that the inciting incident for a marathon is somewhat simple: for a big race like the Walt Disney World Marathon, you've got to pay the registration fee long in advance, before it sells out.

Once I bought my registration, there was no turning back. I was committed to showing up at the starting line, regardless of how hard it might get along the way.

What irreversible step might you be able to take in the direction of the adventure God is calling you to join Him in? Will you dare to take the kind of risks that don't allow you to turn back?

It would be much easier for you to close this book, turn on the TV, and start watching *Hamilton* again. But history has its eyes on you, and the opportunity to live a meaningful journey is only just beginning. Whether this stresses you out or gets you excited, the truth is that the challenge awaiting you is far greater than the attempt to finish Mickey's Kitchen Sink Sundae.

CHAPTER FIVE

Only 189 Feet

So you've taken the steps to ask God for guidance in your story, and you've secured an individual (or two) to be your human guide to keep you on task along the way. Maybe you've even engaged in the inciting incident, moving one step closer to the climactic scene you're excited to embrace.

We will talk about the kinds of conflict you might encounter soon, in the next section—but for now it's important that we think about the continued necessity of keeping our story on track. All of the tools we've talked about already to this point will help us, to be sure...but knowing that humans are easily distracted, we need to hammer this home one last time.

Besides having too many plot lines happening at the same time, another way to ruin a perfectly good movie would be to forget what the plot was supposed to be about, spinning off into a sidetracked mess.

The first *Toy Story* film is essentially a tale about two toys making a long and dangerous journey back to their beloved owner. But can you imagine if Woody and Buzz got to Pizza Planet, only to discover an entire world of characters living inside the arcade games? As they pass an old game called Fix-It Felix, Jr., the camera shifts from following the two toys and begins focusing on the tale of a digital villain named Wreck It Ralph and his companion Vanellope for the final 45 minutes of the film.

By the end, not only are we confused, but we may have somewhat forgotten that the plot was supposed to be about the toys returning to Andy. It's no secret that the Pizza Planet truck makes a hidden cameo in every single Pixar movie, but there's a big difference between a discreet detail and a shifted narrative.

We know and expect that Pixar would never make this kind of error in their stories, because they are master storytellers. In our own personal lives, however, we can allow many factors to drive our story off course—and our endings suffer as a result.

There's a difference between reality and facade, between what will truly bring us lasting peace and that which is only a placeholder or even a distraction. How many times have we had a beautiful ending goal in mind, only to get sidetracked by something that ended up to be, in reality, smoke and mirrors?

To keep us moving in the right direction, let's talk a little bit about castles, magic, and things like chemistry.

In your opinion, what is the most iconic location in all of Walt Disney World? For some, personal memories and special moments may impact your answer, like if you got engaged in front of the Imagination pavilion at EPCOT.

I think for most, the location that comes to mind is one we've already mentioned: none other than Main Street, USA. While there are plenty of amazing places all across the four parks and the rest of the property, there's nothing like coming around the corner of Town Square, looking up the street, and seeing Cinderella Castle for the first time (or the thirtieth time).

It looks massive. It looms large. It invites you to continue moving down Main Street, towards the Hub and therefore your decision of which land to visit next—although simultaneously, Cinderella Castle can cause you to completely forget for a moment the existence of the Haunted Mansion or the line length of Seven Dwarfs Mine Train.

If you had to guess, you might think that Cinderella Castle is the tallest building in all of the Walt Disney

World parks. If you did, you'd be wrong—because at 199.5 feet tall, Expedition Everest gets the gold, followed closely by the Tower of Terror at 199 feet.

If I didn't know any better, I would have thought that Cinderella Castle soared over 200 feet tall, but in actuality, it's only 189 feet high. The feeling that it's such a great height isn't by mistake or accident—it's designed that way on purpose using a trick called forced perspective.

The effect begins when you first turn the corner in Town Square to head down the street. From your vantage point on the ground, the buildings on Main Street will look completely normal...but in reality, the windows get smaller on the second level and even smaller in the buildings that feature a third floor. This tricks your eye into believing the shops and stores are taller than they actually are. When you look down the street to the Castle, the forced perspective of Main Street adds to the illusion within your mind: if these buildings are tall, then the castle must be huge!

Additionally, the same trick is used on the Castle itself. If you were able to measure the stones and windows from the bottom of the Castle moving upwards, you'd find that everything gets smaller as you move to the top. It's tricking your mind into believing immediately upon sight that the structure is much more immense than it actually is.

If you're like me, this kind of knowledge doesn't ruin the magic of Walt Disney World for you. Instead, it adds to the amazement of what the Imagineers have been able to create for guests to experience. While we often talk about Disney in terms of magic and pixie dust, we all know that there's a very real and intelligent process to making the dreams become reality.

Did you know that the majority of the Haunted Mansion ride happens in a nondescript rectangular white building? I know, you wanted to believe it was all taking place inside the big estate you see sitting on the hill. But inside that building is simply the foyer, the stretching room (which you experienced if you've been inside the attraction, it features the four portraits)...and a small break room and bathroom for Mansion Cast Members.

The foyer and room with "no windows and no doors" are visited regularly by guests and the Ghost Host, adorned with the kinds of details you would expect to find within the mansion: creepy flickering lighting and cobwebs. The CM bathroom is a little more modern, opting for florescent bulbs and running water, with no "wall to wall chills" in sight.

I once read a Cast Member's commentary on using this bathroom. That admittedly sounds really strange, but in actuality it's pretty funny to think about. They mentioned that, while sitting in the stall of the normal looking bathroom, all that can be heard are the muffled sounds of what's being repeated on the other side of the wall.

Imagine trying to use the bathroom and hearing "Do not pull down on the safety bar please. *I* will lower it for you." over and over and over again. The Ghost Host is a lot less spooky when he's constantly interrupting what would normally be the privacy of the restroom.

While none of us would envision such a scene taking place inside the gloomy Haunted Mansion, the truth is that the creepy house is nothing more than a facade, housing several purposes inside the same (rather small) space. Cinderella Castle is made of fiberglass, not bricks. The shops on Main Street don't really host piano lessons or photography studios on the upper floors—they're actually offices and conference rooms. Additionally, there's no way to look out of the Main Street windows from those offices. They're just for show.

I've used the word facade twice in this chapter already for a couple of reasons. The first is that it's a somewhat official word used by many inside the Walt Disney Company to describe structures that look one way yet house other purposes within—like the Hollywood Tower Hotel, which we all know doesn't have anything to do with a real hotel at all beyond the storyline of Tower of Terror.

But the other reason I think the word facade is important is because everything we've been talking about for the last few pages is deeply connected to how we live our lives. For some of us, the facade can be built purposefully, specifically, and intentionally. How many times have you built a beautiful disguise around aspects of your life specifically to mask the reality of what's happening within?

This was certainly the case for some of those who lived in the day of Jesus, as we find when he spoke to the Pharisees:

> You Pharisees clean the outside of the cup and dish, but inside you are full of greed and wickedness.
> —Luke 11:39

From outside appearances, the lives of these Pharisees looked as clean and spotless as Main Street, USA. But when someone peeked past their grandiose words and loud prayers, what was uncovered was that they were actually living a facade. All of their supposed religiosity was just preformed like an actor on the stage.

I hope that you don't see yourself reflected in the lives of those Pharisees. If you do, take the steps to break down the masquerade you've constructed as quickly as possible, even though the process will be hard. In the end, you'll be vastly better off by taking those difficult steps.

When it comes to the individual lives of each of you who are reading this book, I want to give you the benefit of the doubt and assume you aren't like the Pharisees. Let's assume you aren't faking matters of faith, and you really do want to do everything necessary to live out in fullness the story that God is inviting you into.

You start heading towards an obvious goal, and the story you're writing seems to have vivid clarity. But then, suddenly, an attractive sounding offer pops up across the screen of your life, tempting you to jump ship and head towards a brand new ending unrelated to where you were previously going. Before you know it, you're swept away faster than the people who click on the ads for BuzzzTube videos in *Ralph Breaks the Internet*.

Let me give you a real-life example of this so you understand what I'm talking about. For over 13 years, I've worked as a part-time youth pastor in the span of 3 different churches. During that time, I've obviously met many teenagers and seen them grow up to different outcomes and futures. Being that my relationship with them was that of a youth pastor to a student within a church setting, matters of faith continuously surfaced week to week.

As you might imagine, there were varied responses from the teens over the years to the offer of a relationship with God and a deeper faith. It might seem that the most frustrating cases would be those who faithfully attended youth group yet continuously rejected the message of Jesus presented each week in the lesson. But in reality, the most frustrating moments are with those who show amazing potential for the Kingdom of God, only to head in another direction when things get tough or busy.

One such specific example, which has happened *countless* times in the last 13 years: A guy begins coming to youth group. At first, the main draw seems to be the active games that we play, like capture the flag: he keeps showing up week after week to compete and have fun. But soon, he is listening closer during the lesson and offering insightful thoughts to the discussion that follows. He's reading his Bible at home on his own, discovering new ideas about his faith and encouraging others to come alongside him in the process. He might even be willing to lead a lesson one week. He begins to consider what this apprenticeship to Jesus might mean for the rest of his life and how his story may become deeper, richer; more meaningful.

But then, like a BuzzzTube ad flashing up on the screen, he notices one of the girls in the youth group (seemingly for the first time). She's witty, she shares some of his musical likes, and the way her eyes sparkle when she laughs is *undeniable*. It isn't long before they're the youth group power couple, attending every single meeting and event hand in hand. They're talking about getting married someday after two strong months of dating, and they're still both talking about their mutual love for Christ.

But then, something goes wrong. For whatever reason, the honeymoon phase of their dating relationship goes south. Maybe they just don't feel as close as they did when things started, or perhaps another person entered the picture and she felt drawn to a third party. Whatever the reason, the relationship ends.

Here's what is unilaterally, consistently certain: they will both fade away from youth group. Every single time this has happened in any of my youth groups, it's had the same outcome. Both of them feel awkward being around their former boyfriend or girlfriend, and so while they might start out coming to a few events or gatherings, they eventually come up with excuses that prevent them from ever coming again.

Youth group isn't the end-all when it comes to a successful faith. But I can also say that (in the case of 99 percent of those teenagers) when they decided to walk away from the youth group, they also totally lost track of whatever dream had begun to form in their minds before the relationship began.

In most of the cases, they said things following the breakup like "I don't know how I'm going to move on" or "I don't have any reason to get up in the morning any more."

Don't get me wrong. I'm not saying dating is bad or having a significant other will ruin your life. I'm happily married, so I obviously know the importance of that phrase in Genesis 2, where God says that it's not good for us to be alone and that we need a "suitable helper".

But how often have we been derailed from life transformation by other kinds of stories—even good sub-plots—that show up in our lives? We would never watch a movie that had such a strange, almost schizophrenic quality about it...but we consistently allow whatever comes along to guide our next steps.

As the lyrics of the band The Gray Havens remind us in their song High Enough: "travel back down the corridor of Eden, see the apple shine...it was gonna be the ladder to the skies in their mind."

In Eden, the forbidden fruit that grew on the tree was the facade. Adam and Eve fully believed the lie that eating the fruit would bring them to a bigger and better under-standing of themselves, the world, and morality. They thought that it was going to be the "ladder to the skies." In the end, it only led to death. It was a flashy, exciting, distraction that took them away from the perfection that they only briefly enjoyed.

When I think about the youth group kids I've encoun-tered over the years, I don't blame any of them for dating. It's a natural and expected part of growing up, and in the best case scenarios it can be the stepping stone to marriage.

But I shake my head at how many of them so quickly put all of their eggs in one basket, believing the lie that if the relationship failed, then everything was pointless.

When we place our whole faith and trust in anything that can falter, we set ourselves up for failure—even if those things are good. If we place our entirety into a good marriage partner, we find ourselves at an end if that person dies. If we're endlessly wrapped up in the comfort of having a safe and stable home, we'll be at our wits end if a fire breaks out and burns it down. If your mental sta-bility is found in feeling the warm Florida sun on your skin as you walk towards Cinderella Castle, then you'll be devastated when a worldwide outbreak like Covid-19 causes a multi-month shutdown of all the parks.

Almost every single one of the people, places, and things around us have the capacity to let us down, either purposefully or via an event that is a result of bad random chance, like a fire or a death.

All of these objects, locations, and individuals are facades in our lives. That doesn't mean that they are necessarily bad in any way, it simply means that they don't have the power to provide unchanging joy and peace within our lives. They are beautiful, enticing, and may even provide something that we need...but it's impossible for them to ever truly fulfill.

We might chuckle at the juvenile choice of the young teens to put all of their passion and devotion into a romance that, as adults, we know is unlikely to last all too long. But how often have we done the exact same thing? How many times have we chosen to put the entirety of our devotion and trust into a facade that failed us? How many times have you been taken off track from your calling by the offer of a story that ended up to bring nothing but pain and misery?

As hard as it may be for some to believe, the only thing that will truly give us peace and a sense of fulfillment is to follow Jesus and embark upon the adventure that He has planned for us. In the end, your house could burn down, loved family members could die, you might face a devastating break up, and you could lose all of the money in your savings account—but God will remain unchanged. His offer of joy and peace will not be shaken in the midst of any of your misfortunes, and His call on your life will not cease to become relevant.

So how do we ensure that we're on the right track? You put Christ and His call first and foremost in your life. This in no way means that you are going to need to ignore your family or set aside your dreams of getting married. It simply means that, if you want to live out the fulfilling adventure God has for you, that you have to examine your priorities and decide to believe that no matter what the future may hold, the story isn't over.

When you decide to commit to the inciting incident in God's story, you're dedicating yourself to something more than a facade. While the specific ending might not be clear at this point, you can be sure that you're not going to get to the last page and find out that you were tricked and everything is actually made of fiberglass.

Take the step, right now, to dedicate yourself to the inciting incident. You won't be limited to 189 feet—you'll be able to endlessly grow taller in your faith and in your partnership with God.

PART III

....

Conflict

CHAPTER SIX

Walt's Folly

It seems to me that people really used to love the word folly. It's a word that I'm not sure I've ever heard used in my lifetime in conversation, yet it pops up in descriptions of perceived failures all throughout the 1940s and 50s.

Essentially, folly means to lack good sense or to be foolish. When presented with a series of options in life, making the decision to choose the one that would lead you to ruin and to become a laughing stock would be folly. It would be ridiculous.

The public described the work of Walt Disney using the word folly at least twice in his lifetime—and both occasions have gone on to be remembered in the history books. The first should be an event that is very familiar to you by now, because it once again involves the release of *Snow White and the Seven Dwarfs*.

Way back in the first chapter, we talked about that winter night with Walt and his team of animators in 1934. That was long before the first scene was drawn for the movie, and by the time the film was eventually finished three years later in 1937, many people waited in eager anticipation to see the masterpiece for themselves in theaters.

Of course, anything new will have its share of critics, and skeptical individuals who thought Walt was making a mistake by producing an 83 minute animated film seemed to show up at every turn. Early on, his brother Roy and his wife Lillian begged him to turn back and not make the film, thinking it would be a financial disaster. I can imagine that their fears were only heightened when Walt mortgaged his own home in order to provide more funds for the creation of the movie, which required an enormous sum to produce.

Hollywood insiders scoffed at the production, calling it "Disney's Folly." In their minds, history would look back on the release of *Snow White* and remember that it was in this moment that Walt's dreaming had gone too far, leading his legacy to fall into an unmanageable disrepair.

But even the negative comments of those inside the movie industry were not the hardest for Walt to receive. After all, as much as those producers may have thought they could predict the failure of the film in advance within their own minds, they could only base that off of their own imagined misperceptions.

For years following, he would remember one anonymous comment he received from a member of his own team. Before the final edits had been made, Walt invited a small crowd of animators to a theatre to view an unfinished version of the movie. The goal was to gage their reactions, receive feedback, and then finish up making the final cuts and edits.

Most of the written comments that he received following the viewing of the film were positive, but one anonymously written note haunted him for years to come. It was only three words, but those words were clear and direct: "stick to shorts." In other words, someone who not only had worked on the project but also had just finished seeing a portion of the film itself was suggesting that he abandon the almost finished movie and return to strictly making the animated short films.

For years following that incident, even after the success of *Snow White and the Seven Dwarfs*, any member of the team who mentioned anything that stood against any of Walt's ideas could expect a response from him: "I bet *you're* the one who wrote 'stick to shorts!'"

There's a great level of humor intended in his response; a way of joking with someone who disagreed. But at the same time, it clearly impacted Walt greatly and weighed on him that someone on his own team didn't agree with his plan for a full length animated film.

In fact, Imagineer John Hench recalls that the comment kept popping up from time to time in *other* similar reviews held amongst early audiences, in films that were previewed long after *Snow White*. It drove Walt crazy that he couldn't figure out the identity of the one individual who, even *after* the success of the first film, would keep repeating the same old rhetoric: "stick to shorts."

While Walt never did discover his rogue detractor, it wasn't a secret amongst some of the other animators— they just didn't tell him. The person who strongly felt that the focus of the company should stick and remain with shorts was none other than Walt's own brother, Roy Disney.

Apparently, he just didn't have the courage or heart to tell Walt face to face. Either that, or due to the fact that his initial face to face advice towards the film (combined along with that of Walt's wife Lillian) had been rejected and thus he felt as if he wouldn't be heard.

Apart from the amusing anecdote of Roy's involvement, the story of "Disney's folly" presents a series of questions that allow us to consider an alternate reality. What if Walt would have listened to his wife or Roy? What if Walt had been discouraged by the insiders in Hollywood? What if he had never started production, or halted midway through when things became difficult?

What would our modern world look like if *Snow White and the Seven Dwarfs* had never been made? With no *Snow White*, there's no *Beauty and the Beast* or *Frozen*. There's likely no Magic Kingdom or EPCOT. In a world where Walt Disney decided to stick to shorts, there's probably not even rival theme parks, like Universal Studios.

This first success was vital to everything that followed; a testament to the power of the butterfly effect, that knowledge that one small choice can shift the course of humanity forever. In the midst of what ended up to be one of his greatest successes, Walt faced a seemingly insurmountable wall of endless conflict.

And yet, he overcame it.

Every single good story involves conflict. Although it's the part of the journey we naturally dislike the most, a story wouldn't be truly meaningful if conflict didn't exist. Some of the outcome may be the same, to be sure, but we often find that overcoming conflict is what makes the story so compelling.

Take, for example, the story of *Aladdin*. It could be possible for us to come up with a version of the story without Jafar that involves Aladdin ending up with Jasmine. While we'd need to creatively figure out how the "street rat" would meet the Princess and how she would fall in love with him and be given approval from her father for the marriage, it could be done. But it would certainly be a much shorter movie...and think about what we would miss out on.

Without Jafar, there's no reason Aladdin would find himself in the Cave of Wonders. If there's no Cave of Wonders, there's no lamp. And if there's no lamp...there's no Genie.

Need I go on? Without conflict, the ending isn't as amazing, and the climactic scene loses some or all of it's luster. We might still be happy that Aladdin gets to end up with Princess Jasmine, but considering there has been little to no effort getting to that point, that finale doesn't feel "earned."

This isn't just the case in films or fictional stories. Consider one of the most famous passages in all of the Bible, Exodus 3 through 15. It's here that we read about the Israelites in slavery to the evil Egyptian Pharaoh, while a man with a speech impediment (Exodus 4:10) named Moses is called to demand their freedom. After ten plagues and a series of denials, a frustrated and broken Pharaoh agrees to give the people their freedom.

But what if we could consolidate all of that to one chapter? What if Moses would have appeared before Pharaoh that first time and said his famous line: "This is what the LORD, the God of Israel, says: 'Let my people go!'" (Exodus 5:1) only to have Pharaoh respond with: "I don't see a reason why not. Your people are freed!"

We could jump right to chapter 16, which begins to tell us about the Israelites' journey through the desert. The end result, the freedom of the slaves, would be the same—but without the conflict in the middle leading to that freedom, we aren't as amazed at the power of God to overcome the strength of Pharaoh.

There would be no Passover, one of the most important holidays on the Jewish calendar which the Jewish people still celebrate every single year to this day.

Conflict, although potentially evil or negative in itself, is a central part of every meaningful story. While God may not have personally caused the conflict you will experience, we have to realize that God uses all conflict—even evil—to accomplish His ultimate purposes of a beautiful ending. To use the metaphor, what we might see solely as animal feces can be turned around and used as manure to produce crops for consumption.

The manure still looks and smells the same, but now it has been used by someone who can turn something bad into something life giving.

Make no mistake: you will face conflict no matter what kind of life you choose. If you're lazy, sitting on the couch every day with no plans to engage in anything meaningful or to even get a job, you're going to end up encountering the kind of conflict that sounds like a call from your landlord telling you that you're being evicted for not paying rent.

If you are following the call of God in your life, you'll still need to prepare for problems. The question isn't so much about *if* we will face conflict or even what *kind* of conflict we might expect, although those are important to consider. The biggest question we can ask ourselves in advance is "how will I react when conflict arrives?"

How would conflict and the potential of failure impact your journey? Would it encourage you to work even harder, as it seems it did to Walt? Alternatively, would it slow you down in your progress and cause things to move on a much more gradual timeline than you had dreamed?

Because conflict is uncomfortable, and obviously none of us want to experience failure, many of us are often guilty of jumping right into the midst of the story without counting the cost or stopping to consider either of those possibilities. We want to stay focused on the exciting idea that God has given us, not the bad things that could happen along the way. To some degree, this is the right line of thinking—our eyes should be set on the finish line, fixed on the climactic scene that will continue to drive us forward.

At the same time, many experience shock and a deep dismay when they do run into trouble. We assume that since God has called us to be a part of whatever the adventure entails, it must undoubtedly mean that we will face nothing but clear skies, green lights, and open doors moving forward...but that's far from reality.

If we aren't prepared for the potential problems that await us, we set ourselves up for trouble. Sadly, many have allowed failures and complications to define their entire story—and in certain cases, their entire lives. Because a handful of people told them it was impossible, they stopped trying...or due to a mistake being made, the dream was put on the shelf permanently. When the failure defines people, the adventure can be abandoned.

I mentioned some time ago a Disney dream that many fans share in common: to work at Walt Disney World as a Cast Member. But what if someone found themselves accepted into the college program with an illusion that every single moment of their employment would be nothing but Mickey bars and firework shows?

From reading enough books in the series *Earning Your Ears*, it's easy to see that the pixie dust of working for the Walt Disney Company can wear off really quickly. There are currently twelve installments in this series, each of them different diaries written by various cast members who share their experiences. All of the stories are different and from the unique perspectives of the individual who wrote them, but they all share a comment thread: working at any of the theme parks can get stressful.

When you're assigned to work the grill at Pecos Bill Tall Tale Inn and Cafe, sweating and rushing around pulling meat off the hot surface...it can be easy to momentarily forget your proximity to the dazzling Cinderella Castle.

Or maybe you're able to secure a job "making the magic happen" in Guest Services in the City Hall building on Main Street. You'll quickly find out that it takes a lot of sweat, tears, and getting yelled at by angry guests to keep that magic alive. (If you need convincing of the amount of hardships you'd need to face working in Guest Services, I highly recommend reading *Would You Like Magic With That?* by Anne Salisbury.)

In other words, the dream job of being a Cast Member involves a lot of a conflict. It's a lot more stressful than you might think to pursue, accomplish, and achieve that lifelong goal. But anything worth doing is worth struggling through...and what many end up realizing in the end is that the journey is just as important as the destination.

If you're paying close attention, you might have noticed that I mentioned at the beginning of this chapter that people used the word folly to describe Walt Disney's work twice—but so far I've only told you about one.

Of all the words we might consider using when thinking about Disneyland, folly is not one that rises to the top of any list. Yet as Walt promised the public in 1954 that his park would be open within the following year, that's exactly what Hollywood said. As costs continued to mount for Disneyland and as heads of other popular amusement parks began to predict a massive failure for the project, they openly announced that this was "Walt's folly."

Apparently they hadn't learned their lesson during the *Snow White* predictions about applying the word "folly" to one of Walt's projects.

But while the release and overwhelming response of *Snow White and the Seven Dwarfs* immediately alleviated any possible concerns Walt may have had about the film, the opening day of Disneyland only made things worse.

Walt stayed true to his promise that his park would open within a year, and on July 17, 1955, the gates were opened to a pre-invited crowd for the first time. The only problem was that the park wasn't finished...which led to a litany of increasingly worrying problems on what the employees later called "Black Sunday."

It was the worst day in the history of the Walt Disney Company, including the recent losses during the corona virus outbreak. There is seemingly no end to the list of issues that plagued Black Sunday, but I'll mention a few here, each one more disturbing than the last:

The first "adventure" was getting to the park itself. Reports say that there were so many potential guests looking to visit that the traffic backed up all the way to the highway, causing a 7 mile long gridlock. People waited so long that families were forced to relieve themselves on the side of the highway or on the side of Disneyland's parking lot once they finally arrived.

While executives had sent tickets to and invited 15,000 people to explore the new park, they didn't expect people to make counterfeit tickets—but an extravagant amount did, soaring the attendance of those through the gates to almost double what was planned (with over 28,000 entering the normal way). For those who wanted to be a little more adventurous with entry, they could pay $5 to some shady capitalist who had set up his ladder by one of the park's fences.

Because of the unexpected influx of visitors, Cast Members working restaurants and snack stations found themselves quickly running out of food and drinks for guests. Oh, and the water fountains didn't work because Walt had to make a choice before opening day whether to finish them or the restrooms. He chose the bathrooms.

The lack of drinks might have been okay on a cool day, but this was one of the hottest July days on record. The heat soared to 100 degrees. The recently poured asphalt became melted and sticky, causing more than a few women to get their high heels stuck in the black tar on Main Street. I don't know who would want to wear high heels for a day of walking around at Disneyland, so perhaps this one is on them...but when you visit a theme park, you at the *very least* expect to be able to walk on the pathways without having a problem.

At least there were the rides, right? Well...kind of. A handful of the rides were still under construction, and the attractions that were supposed to be open kept breaking down all day long—some worse than others. 36 cars from the Autotopia crashed due to unsafe driving. The Mark Twain Riverboat sank into the Rivers of America due to too many passengers, and some guests had to wade through the water to get to safety. A circus themed parade on Main Street featuring a real tiger and panther became horror when the animals broke free and began engaging in a bloody battle with each other. (For more on this, check out *The Magic Kingdom: Walt Disney and the American Way of Life* by Steven Watts.)

I wish I could say I was joking, because it sounds too insane to be true. But I can guarantee that everything I've just reported is a part of Disneyland history. Someone might use the phrase "dumpster fire" when talking about the failings of those opening days at Disneyland...but at least there were no real fires.

Actually, come to think of it, there was. A gas leak caused temporary closures in Adventureland, Fantasyland, and Frontierland—and a fire to break out on the outside walls of Sleeping Beauty's Castle. Literally, Sleeping Beauty's Castle was *on fire.*

Things were so insane that Walt (who, by the way, accidentally locked himself in his apartment above the Fire Station) didn't even realize the Castle had been on fire until the following day. As the founder of The Walt Disney Company, how crazy do your immediate surroundings have to be for it to take 24 hours for you to find out that your main focal point of all of Disneyland was aflame?!

What a laundry list of failures. With this high a level of mistakes and ridiculous mishaps, it wouldn't have been surprising if Walt would have given up. Of course, Disneyland had already been built by this point, so there was a great level of money, time, and heart put into the park...but how often have so many of us given up when we found ourselves facing far lesser conflicts?

Yet we know the ending of the story. Many decades later, we still shake our heads at the outrageous nature of Black Sunday and the weeks that followed. Yet today we see a thriving Disneyland, an entire "Florida Project," massive animation and live action film studios, and much more.

Late Imagineer and Professor Randy Pausch famously said that "the brick walls aren't there to keep you out. The brick walls are there for you to prove how badly you want something." (Check out Randy's book, *The Last Lecture*, for some more amazing thoughts on living meaningfully.)

On this end of the story, we know that those seeming moments of failure were all worth going through. Are you willing to face the kind of conflict it will take to get to the ending that God's been dreaming about with you? Will you continue through the brick walls of life to prove how badly you want to achieve the climactic scene? Or will you let your failings define your future?

Sure, you might encounter people who see the moments of conflict in your story and define it as folly. You may face those who think they know better telling you to abandon the adventure.

But now, you know better.

Now we know that pushing through conflict is the very means to the victorious ending.

CHAPTER SEVEN

Run the Mile You're In

It's one thing talking about facing conflict, but it's another thing to actually live through it. There are various levels of conflict—some of them easier than others to encounter and survive.

I use that word "survive" purposefully, because the deepest kinds of conflict involve sadness, grief, and pain on a spiritual, guttural level. It's somewhat easy to face losing a job if you have a better one lined up on the horizon. The stress of a seeming failure, like Black Sunday at Disneyland, can fade in the following days when growing crowds continue to attend your park and all of the mistakes with the attractions are fixed.

But what about the kind of conflict that often enters our story unexpectedly, with a disturbing element of grim surprise? How could we prepare ourselves for the tragedy of having a loved one die or experiencing the trauma of abuse?

When it comes to modernity (especially in the United States of America, of which I am a citizen), we have been taught that sorrow and tears are a sign of weakness. This is an especially prevalent ideology amongst men, who are told phrases like "man up" or "act like a man" when any type of emotion is shown.

In my time as a Pastor, I've been asked to oversee many funerals. All of the funerals have been different in many ways, from music styles chosen to the order of the service and what the family decides regarding the location of the viewing. Despite all of these differences, though, I've seen one common thread, a phrase that seems to be mentioned at every single funeral I've ever been a part of officiating.

When a friend or family member gets up front to share a memory or sing a song, they find themselves overcome with emotion and struggling to continue forward. They'll then say to themselves and those gathered: "I'm sorry. I told myself I wouldn't cry when I was doing this."

Your father just died. Your friend is no longer with us in this earthly world. Your daughter overdosed in the midst of an addiction. And yet, you feel like you need to apologize because you started to cry during your speech?

Don't get me wrong, I'm not blaming anyone who has said that phrase—I'm blaming our culture for making us feel as if we should say we're sorry when we grieve. It's true that the easiest thing to do in the midst of horrifying conflict is to ignore it, to suppress it, to sprinkle it with pixie dust and hope that it will pass over us quickly.

In Christian circles, some have been taught a similar type of theology. Some believers have been told that they shouldn't ask questions of God; that to wonder why bad things have happened (and God's possible involvement in them) would be to somehow show a lack of faith in Him.

In reality, nothing could be further from the truth. How do I know that questioning evil in our world and God's seeming silence during times of pain is okay? Because it's exactly what we see all throughout the Scriptures.

In the middle of the Bible is a collection of ancient songs called the Psalms. While the Psalms are often thought about in terms of encouragement, peace, and worship, there is much to be said within their pages regarding the questions on our planet that seem unanswered.

Consider a few excerpts from the Psalms, where David sings questions to God in the midst of his suffering:

> How long, O LORD? Will you forget me forever?
> How long will you hide your face from me?

How long must I wrestle with my thoughts and every day have
sorrow in my heart?
How long will my enemy triumph over me?
—Psalm 13:1-2

Why, O LORD, do you stand far off?
Why do you hide yourself in times of trouble?
—Psalm 10:1

There's even a passage where the author admits to God:
You have made me see troubles, many and bitter.
—Psalm 71:20

The questions that plague the text of Scripture are questions involving God's presence (like "Why have you forsaken me?") and questions about His love (such as "If You really love me, and I am following Your ways, why am I sick?").

Many of us, if we're honest, have found ourselves following that same pattern and wondering about those same types of questions. When someone we love dies—especially if they die young, we wonder why God didn't intervene and allow them to live a full life. When we look around and see bad things happening to us, yet our grouchy atheist neighbor is living life on easy street, we ask ourselves why God would allow someone who believes in him to face hardships if in fact He truly loves us.

These questions—questions of His presence and His love—are all over the Scriptures, but they're also all over the highs and lows of our lives.

I wish I could tell you that when you decide to follow after Jesus, everything gets easier and that you'll experience smooth sailing from that point forward. That would certainly be the most comfortable life to offer, but it wouldn't be the truth.

Jesus himself admitted to His followers the real truth about what we can expect in following after Him: "In this world you will have trouble." (John 16:33) He warns that His disciples could be hated, proclaiming "I have chosen you out of the world. That is why the world hates you."

(John 17:19) Later on, after the resurrection, Jesus cryptically says to the Apostle Peter: "When you are old you will stretch out your hands, and someone else will dress you and lead you where you do not want to go." (John 21:18)

Later in his life, Peter finally discovered what the tragic comment meant. Early Christian historians report that Simon Peter was arrested and crucified by Rome—upside down, due to Peter's own request that he was not worthy to die in the same way as Christ. For Peter, deciding to follow Jesus ultimately ended up in him literally getting killed in one of the worst ways imaginable.

This deserves a full stop. I mean, this is the antithesis of every single feeling I get when I'm walking through Walt Disney World. When I'm on Disney property, I feel like I'm at home; I feel like I'm safe. There's nothing more comforting than the smell of cookies coming out of the Main Street Bakery as I walk towards Cinderella Castle in the morning. The kind of danger I like to face is the safe kind, the kind I know my stomach will feel as I plunge down the mountainside on Expedition Everest.

It's almost laughable typing (or for you, reading) those words right now in the midst of what Peter faced, isn't it? As a follower of Jesus in the 21st century, I'm programmed to seek comfort; I'm addicted to safety and security.

Yet there are times when the pixie dust fades, those horrifying moments of reality in which we are reminded that this world is actually full of many hard and sorrowful days that we must all face.

It's those moments that remind me of my journey during the running of the Walt Disney World Marathon that I mentioned earlier. There was nothing comfortable about the run, and I didn't feel that familiar sense of security that I had become accustomed to while entering each of the parks. The longer the race stretched on, the more my legs seemed to seize up—rendering any running impossible and my only option to shuffle forward awkwardly. The final stretch of the race occurs through World Showcase in EPCOT, and I was barely able to make it all the way around to Mexico.

I'm not sure if Paul, the author of much of the New Testament, was a runner or not, but he seemed to be familiar with this kind of a painful struggle. In many of his writings, he takes the tension of running a long race and turns it into a metaphor for something even more important: living a meaningful life.

Here's a few of his excerpts:

> Let us lay aside every weight, and sin which clings so closely, and let us run with endurance the race that is set before us.
> —Hebrews 12:1

> Do you not know that in a race all the runners run, but only one receives the prize? So run that you may obtain it. Every athlete exercises self-control in all things. They do it to receive a perishable wreath, but we an imperishable. So I do not run aimlessly.
> —1 Corinthians 9:24-27

> One thing I do: forgetting what lies behind and straining forward to what lies ahead, I press on toward the goal for the prize of the upward call of God in Christ Jesus.
> —Philippians 3:13-14

Even near the end of his life while in prison in Rome (in what was probably the last letter he ever wrote), Paul couldn't help but give one final running metaphor:

> I have fought the good fight, I have finished the race, I have kept the faith.
> —2 Timothy 4:7-9

We've been told that to grieve is weak; to avoid pain and suffering at all costs. Some televangelists have even claimed that the Bible promises prosperity, health, and wealth to anyone who follows Jesus. But those are false teachings, opposing realities to what we actually see within the pages of Scripture.

The good news of the Bible on grief is so much better than the message of the television preachers who claimed we would never have to face hardship. If that's actually what the Bible said, we would all likely find ourselves doubting that it could ever be true every single time we encounter a difficult reality in our world.

But no—as we've seen, Scripture (and Jesus) are brutally honest about the hard nature of "running this race" called life. The resounding message of the Bible is not that will face zero hard times, but instead that we can be encouraged to keep moving forward towards the finish line in the midst of the cramps, the pains, and the stressors.

If you're human, you'll face grief. But the Scriptures claim that you're not alone in the middle of it.

My friend Rick is a runner too, but he's not a runner like me. As I said, I'm the kind of runner who limped to the finish line during the Walt Disney World Marathon. Rick is the kind of guy who signed up and completed the Dopey Challenge (running a 5k, 10k, half marathon, and full marathon at the parks all in a series of 4 consecutive days) without batting an eye.

Oh, and he ran the half in a Tweedledum costume alongside his friend, who was dressed as Tweedledee.

As I write this, he's just completed day 244 in a running streak—meaning that he has not missed a day of running for over half of a year. Those of you who read my earlier stories of the Marathon and thought "I would never want to run that far, for any reason, ever," are now experiencing a new level of incredulity.

I don't know how many marathons he has completed within his life, because twenty-six miles is essentially just another name for "Saturday's brisk jog" for Rick. I do know that I'll never forget a lesson he taught me after he completed the Nashville Marathon in 2017. It was in the aftermath of yet another successfully crossed finished line that he was hit with the reality of the struggles of the race of life.

Here's Rick in his own words, written for his blog during that dark time:

I had grand plans, friends, to write this blog. In fact, I've been taking notes about this entry for months. I was going to return from Nashville, triumphant from having set a new marathon personal best, with a new Western hat and funny yet poignant stories about my friends and travel companions. I was going to tell you about how the things I love to do, some of my passions, mostly involve taking my time.

Marriage.

Marathons.

Brewing beer.

Bread-making.

Baseball.

Relationships.

I was even going to quote David Bowie ("Time may change me/But I can't trace time.")

But to misquote my friend Robert Burns, "The best-laid plans of mice and men go often awry." (As a former high school English teacher, of course I know the line is actually "The best laid schemes o' Mice an' Men/Gang aft agley".)

See, within ninety minutes of arriving home from a terrific trip to Nashville, my mother called to tell me my 18-year old nephew had been killed in a car accident.

And now time grinds to a halt.

The kindness of people continues to overflow when they ask what they can do to help. My answer is always the same: Speed up time to get to the easier part. Of course that's not possible, and while it's beautiful to see friends and family support one another with presence and prayer, our heartache continues because we love Evan.

Just this morning a dear friend called me, and all I could talk about was my family's faith, our faith in Jesus, in the Comforter/Advocate that is the Holy Spirit. "It seems so incongruous to say we know God will sustain us, and yet we remain so heart-broken. But these things coexist within us all. And praise God for it. And dammit." All at the same time.

And so maybe these thoughts all work together, after all. During the race in Nashville, a spectator held a sign that read "Run the mile you're in." Most days I would say that sounds trite, too simplistic, and maybe a little corny. But just like persevering through what was a difficult marathon, maybe it's the best way to mourn my nephew, my buddy, an inspiration to many, little Genghis Khan, a young man of God.

Rather than speed through this, we need to be present and run the mile we're in.

My friend Rick's story continues to inspire me, not because he completed the Nashville marathon, but because he took the hard road and endured through the pain of losing his nephew. While his hope would have been to speed up time, he knew the most important path he could possibly take would be to purposefully live in the present.

Once again, that's also the message of Scripture: be present in pain and endure moments of hardship knowing that God is alongside you and actively working to redeem and restore. Don't focus on the past of mile four and don't get ahead of yourself by thinking you might not make it to mile twenty-six. You can run the mile you're in, even when it's hard, knowing that there are not always clear-cut answers...but that God sits in the sadness alongside you.

It's the clear message of the Psalms as they turn a corner and continue on from the earlier moments of darkness:

> But I will trust in your unfailing love; my heart rejoices in your salvation.
>
> —Psalm 13:5

> But you, O God, do see trouble and grief; you consider it to take it in hand. The victim commits himself to you; you are the helper of the fatherless.
>
> —Psalm 10:14

> You will restore my life again; from the depths of the earth you will again bring me up. You will increase my honor and comfort me once again.
>
> —Psalm 71:20-21

And remember that quote from Jesus, where he told his followers to expect trouble as they navigate the world? It turns out that there's comforting news there as well:

> I have told you these things, so that in me you may have peace. In this world you will have trouble. But take heart! I have overcome the world.
>
> —John 16:33

Jesus knew the mission, loving God and loving people, was going to involve vast amounts of difficult conflict. But Jesus also promised that he was right alongside us in the midst of those difficulties.

You won't need to go looking for conflict because, to your dismay, most of the time it will find you. Yet as you run with purpose the mile of life you find yourself in, take heart in the knowledge that Jesus is running alongside you.

You *can* finish the adventure and cross the finish line.

CHAPTER EIGHT

The Positive Negatives

I know...*another* chapter on conflict?! It's the least exciting portion of our adventure, and yet as we've learned it is an essential, meaningful, transformative part of every single story. It makes sense that it's the longest conversation we'll have in this book, because conflict takes up the majority of our adventure here on Earth. In addition to that truth, we now have established that the Scriptures have a clear and concise theology of being present in pain and continuing to run the race in the midst of hardships.

But there's one last piece to the puzzle when it comes to conflict, and it once again involves a question of God's presence. If something truly bad does happen, is there any redemption or good that could come as a result?

In other words, it's comforting to know that God is present in our pain, but it would be even more reassuring to know that He wasn't just sitting idly by, shrugging His shoulders sadly as if nothing could be done.

Consider the saddest scenes in the classic films that we all know and love. I know we're talking about fictional movies here, but there are some really painful moments represented in many of them that reveal things about our own journeys—which is why we connect with them.

In *The Lion King*, young Simba has to deal with the loss of not only his father, but the loss of everything that his father Mufasa represented to him: his trainer on how to successfully one day be King, his protector, and his guide.

In *Big Hero 6*, fourteen year old Hiro has to grapple with the death of his older brother Tadashi, which he learns was anything but an accident.

During *Toy Story 2*, we see a flashback that reveals how Jessie was abandoned by her former owner, Emily. Now, even years later, Jessie still struggles with anxiety over being abandoned and left behind.

Over in a galaxy far, far away, during the final events of *Revenge of the Sith*, Obi-Wan Kenobi must come to grips with the reality that his loved apprentice, Anakin Skywalker, has betrayed him and has become a Sith Lord. The hearts of *Star Wars* fans everywhere break when he shouts the tearful lines: "You were the Chosen One! It was said that you would destroy the Sith, not join them! Bring balance to the force, not leave it in darkness! You were my brother, Anakin! I loved you."

Sure, these are fictional characters living through scenarios that never really happened within the course of human history. Lions can't talk, toys aren't secretly alive, and there is no such thing as a volcano planet called Mustafar.

But how many of us can relate to losing a parent at a young age? Or maybe someone close to you has been killed due to the reckless (or intentional) actions of another person, leaving you with feelings of wanting revenge. Maybe you were abandoned by a spouse or betrayed by a friend, and you feel like you may never be able to trust anyone ever again.

Yes, they're fictional characters who never existed and who will never exist. Yet they've experienced things on the screen that many of us we are all too familiar with.

If and when these things happen to us (which they undoubtedly have and will), we return to our original question from the beginning of the chapter: is God doing anything as far as redeeming these negative situations?

In the stories we've looked at, it's easy to see how good ultimately comes out on top. Within a maximum of two hours, we're able to see everything coming to a happily ever after, and we know that when everything is said and done, light has had the final word over darkness. Even in the midst of a seemingly dark ending like *Revenge of the Sith*, we know that *A New Hope* is right around the corner that will make the wrongs right again.

In our own lives, though, it can be difficult to imagine anything good at all coming from these types of events—even when we acknowledge the fact that conflict is in the midst of every story.

During my life, I have been through all sorts of various hardships like the ones we've been discussing...but the event that changed my life began on December 14th, 2005, when my fifteen year old brother Nick was diagnosed with leukemia, a cancer of the blood.

Up to that point, our family had finished up Thanksgiving celebrations and was looking forward to spending Christmas together with friends and loved ones. My parents undoubtedly had gone shopping for gifts to place under the tree, snow may have been in the northeast Ohio air, and cheerful and familiar tunes were playing over the radio. Until December 14th, everything seemed normal.

After that date, everything changed and would never be the same again. Instead of coming downstairs on Christmas morning for a cozy and relaxed time with family in the comfort of our own home, we were forced to open gifts within a hospital room at St. Jude Hospital in Memphis, Tennessee.

As wonderful as St. Jude Children's Hospital was and is, it didn't come close to comparing to home—especially with my brother's fight against cancer in the midst of everything. Things were visibly and unarguably different in a vast array of ways.

For the next eight months, my mom and brother lived at St. Jude while the rest of us had to return to our "normal" lives in Ohio. I continued my sophomore year of college, my sister went on with her junior year of high school, and my dad continued working for the Metroparks to provide income for the entire family. When holidays allowed for extended time away from our duties, we would all load up in the family mini van and make the several hour trip to Memphis, excited to reunite as a whole group once more.

Looking back, I suppose it was a strange time...but in the midst of the conflict, it became our average, everyday life. There were many reminders of the strangeness of this "new reality," though—like returning from spring break and hearing the stories of others who had been to a beach or a backpacking trip. That stood in stark contrast to my break, which was spent in and out of the hospital.

During a visit that summer in August of 2006, Nick faced an upcoming bone marrow transplant, the latest strategy scheduled to fight the leukemia in his blood. As he considered the implications of this next step and the uncertainty of his future, he wrote to his friends back home on his Xanga blog:

> I am still really scared and I have no clue what is going to happen, but I know that God has an awesome plan for me. Everybody keep me in your prayers, and meanwhile I'll still be singing: "Spirit take me up in arms with you.

At the time he typed out those lyrics to Switchfoot's song *Twenty-four* in the final line of his blog, there was no way he could have known that he would die 23 days later. Although we all knew the severity and seriousness of his diagnosis, none of us expected that just a few weeks after writing these words he would suffer a brain bleed, become unconscious, and pass away.

In retrospect, we might look at the story and sadly shake our heads at the unfulfilled hope that my brother wrote about in early August. After all, he was convinced that God had an "awesome plan" for him, and yet he died...how could that be even a remotely good plan by any stretch of the imagination?

Is there anything in the Scripture that speaks to this kind of devastating conflict? Is there any story that involves a person having to endure vast amounts of trouble, yet (more importantly) eventually saw good that came from their experiences?

There are several stories like this, but let's just talk about two of them. The first is found at the end of the first book in the Bible, a book called Genesis. By chapter 37, we're introduced to an annoying seventeen year old named Joseph, who tells his brothers about the dreams he's had which depict his entire family bowing down to him. Joseph is convinced that these dreams actually mean something; that they aren't just the after-effects of eating too close to bedtime.

As much of a pest as Joseph seems at the beginning of the story, we wouldn't wish upon him the kinds of things he is forced to experience shortly afterward. His brothers, tired of his shenanigans, decide to sell him into slavery to some passing travelers, who in turn sell him to Egypt's captain of the guard.

Things seem to be going as well as they could possibly go for Joseph when he is approached by the wife of the captain of the guard, who has noticed that he's handsome and thus would like to spend some "alone time" with him while her husband is out working. Joseph refuses and runs off—but she's furious that he denied her and so she decides to falsely accuse him of attempted rape.

Faced with a choice between his slave and his wife, the captain of the guard chooses to take the side of his wife... and Joseph is thrown into prison as an innocent man. Now he's not only a slave far from home, he's a prisoner as well.

It seems like there could be no possible redemption in the sad story of this man, but as he's living in the jail, he has the chance to reveal to the Pharaoh (the King over all of Egypt) the truth about a concerning vision. For the next seven years, Joseph says, there will be an abundance of food—but the seven years following those will be seven years of famine. Joseph urges the Pharaoh to begin planning now, during the good years, to prepare for the bad ones to come.

Pharaoh believes him, and not only is Joseph released from prison, he is also made second in command in Egypt to oversee the entire system of storing the provisions. Eventually, when the seven years of famine have begun, Joseph's brothers are required to travel to Egypt and appear before Joseph himself to ask for assistance in the form of food, although they don't recognize him after all the years of separation.

Eventually, after the truth comes out, the brothers realize they could find themselves in big trouble. Joseph wields a lot of power in the position he has now found himself in, and he could have them killed in an act of retribution just by saying the word.

Instead, Genesis 50:20 records the response of Joseph to his brothers looking back on everything that happened to him:

> You intended to harm me, but God intended it for good to accomplish what is now being done, the saving of many lives.

In the end, Joseph looked at the strange series of events and misfortunes that had characterized his life and connected all the dots. If his brothers hadn't tried to harm him by selling him into slavery, he would never have been in Egypt. If he wasn't in Egypt, he wouldn't have been in jail, which means he would never have had the chance to talk to Pharaoh about the visions. And if he hadn't done that...the famine would have been a surprise, no food would have been stored in preparation, and countless lives would have been lost.

For Joseph, there was no denying the evil, grief, sadness, and pain—but he simultaneously saw the deeper reality of God, who decided to use that evil intent in a way that would actually save lives and restore communities.

In a shorter narrative over in the book of Ruth, we're introduced to an old woman named Naomi who becomes a widow only three verses into the story. After her husband dies, she is supported in her grief for ten years by her two sons...who then die just as abruptly as their father.

With all of her blood relatives gone, Naomi is left with nothing but her two daughters-in-law for her future. In an ancient world where women were afforded very little rights, this wasn't good news. It's not like all of the women could take up extra shifts at work to make up for the lost income—the ancient Middle East was ruled by men, and women without a man to make a way for them were often left by the wayside.

When Naomi hears that a famine has ended in her home country, she longs for at least a semblance of normality, and so she decides to head home. Ruth, her daughter-in-law, decides to make the trip with her and support as best she can.

When the two arrive back in Bethlehem, old friends are excited to see the return of their long lost neighbor. They call out to her using her name, which seems like a safe bet...but as they yell "Naomi," she's only thinking about the meaning of her name: pleasant.

In the midst of the others shouting "pleasant," she announces that she sadly no longer wants to be called by a name that equates to anything happy. Instead, she's decided to change her name to Mara, which means bitter. She goes on to explain that she's seen nothing but bitterness and misfortune over the course of the last 10 years, and thus she's willing to essentially accept her fate of a hard life with open arms.

As far as the story goes, it seems as if Naomi (I guess I should say Mara) is putting a period on the end of the sentence that is her life. It looks like she has come to the conclusion that there's no hope for any redemption or future joy in her narrative.

Yet the story continues, and in her newfound home Ruth goes out to pick leftover grain from the fields. This was a way to support the poor in the community, a law from God written in Deuteronomy 4:19-22. Even in an ancient world where women were considered less than second class, this was one of the many ways that God was requiring people to advance past their limited viewpoints.

During her time gathering grain the fields, she meets a man named Boaz, and they eventually get married. The majority of the book is devoted to telling about how the couple meets, how their relationship evolves, and what happens following the wedding. Things progress as they often do, and soon Ruth finds herself giving birth to a baby boy.

In the midst of what could be seen as a simple love story between Ruth and Boaz that ends "happily ever after," many who were paying attention at the beginning of the story still wonder about the sadness of Naomi. Did she get a happy ending? Was there any redemption for the woman who decided that she would accept a life of bitterness?

In the final scene, we see her holding her grandson for the first time—a beautiful moment for any grandparent, but especially in the life of Naomi, who had experienced so much death. They named her grandson Obed, a name which means servant of God—a reference to the fact that he would serve his grandmother and provide for her when he grew up.

The ending of the book of Ruth is (at face value) just a simple family tree genealogy. The final 6 verses seem to present a long and somewhat boring list of names leading up to Boaz: Perez was the father of Hezron, Hezron the father of Ram, and so on until we get to Boaz himself. Then we see his son Obed's name, followed by a few others:

> Obed was the father of Jesse, and Jesse the father of David.
> —Ruth 4:22

That's where the story ends. To the modern eye, this list of names might not mean much—but to the ancient reader, this is huge. The David on this list isn't just any average David who lived over 3,000 years ago...he is King David, the one who famously faced Goliath; the David who to this day is a central and revered figure in Jewish history.

There's two things inferred here regarding Naomi: firstly, that she was related to King David—an even more significant relation in a culture where honor depended upon the legacy of your descendants. But more importantly, we learn from Matthew that 28 generations after David, Jesus was born into the same family.

In other words, Naomi is eventually found in the ancestry of Jesus. This was a woman who, years earlier in the story, had wanted to change her name to Bitter because there seemed to be no way she would ever experience any kind of pleasantness ever again. She probably didn't live long enough to see her relation to David, and she definitely didn't live until the birth of the long awaited Christ.

But I can almost guarantee that she never expected that thousands of years later we would still be talking about her, sharing the results of her legacy. She thought her story was over; a tragic yet forgettable life in the course of history— and yet it was far from being the final chapter.

Once again, the Scriptures show us not some perfected and skewed version of reality, where no one faces any hardships, but instead a picture of deep grief and pain that we all know exists in this world. But then we are met with the knowledge of how God works in the midst of it to redeem and restore all things. It doesn't reduce or change the pain of the other loss, but it does create a clear message: God can and will still work in all things "for the good of those who love Him." (Romans 8:28)

Every time we watch a Pixar movie for the first time, we can undoubtedly expect to experience heart-wrenching scenes that will cause us to cry—but we know that there are amazing writers who are going to take that initial pain and turn it around by the final scene. In the end, we're still crying...but this time for good reasons. In *Up*, we still miss Ellie and wish her and Carl could have lived forever, but we are filled with great hope about the future of Carl and Russell. A new beautiful chapter of life begins.

That's essentially the message of the Scripture. There is an amazing Writer authoring our story, and as we discover and encounter scenes of pain we can find some kind of peace in knowing that there is hope for the future. It may not be the same ever again—but there is still a new and beautiful chapter available, perhaps even one that "saves many lives."

Fourteen years after the tragedy of losing my brother, my family has been able to see some of the "awesome plan" that Nick was so convinced of before he died. For the two years immediately following, we were invited back to the campus of St. Jude in Memphis for a "Day of Remembrance," a series of events, services, and reunions with doctors and nurses, as well as other families who had also lost their child within those prior two years.

Although the event was great and certainly needed for the grieving families, it left a hole in that next third year. Besides these two events, there seemed to be very little support for parents and siblings who had lost their loved one coming from the hospital. The focus was on treating and supporting the children who still were in the midst of their battle with cancer, which of course makes sense as that's the main purpose of a hospital to begin with.

But as time went on, grieving families and the decision makers at St. Jude Hospital became increasingly convinced that something more needed to be done. Not only were bereaved siblings and parents lacking the support needed following a death—the doctors and nurses who had established relationships with the kids as their patients needed increased support as well.

In 2010, my mom Wendy was invited by St. Jude to join a focus group with 12 other parents who were seeking to address these kinds of challenges. After a few years of getting started in the right direction, the focus group evolved into a more official Steering Council, hiring a Bereavement Coordinator for the first time.

For the next 9 years, Wendy flew from Ohio to Memphis on a monthly basis to help shape and guide the new efforts in supporting grieving individuals and families. There are a lot of amazing things that have happened over the course of those years and many lives have been positively affected, but I think overall there is one thing that stands out to me the most in the midst of them all: the arc of my mom's story and how a negative turn ended up becoming the catalyst to the *saving of many lives*.

Joseph had the opportunity to save people from the famine, literally keeping them from death. With any conversation involving grief, I think it's more than possible that the now established Quality of Life department of St. Jude has steered individuals away from the possibility of suicide.

But in another sense, many lives are being saved emotionally and mentally as well. With a strong support system offered through the hospital, people all around the world are receiving the assistance needed to continue moving forward and running the mile they find themselves in within their story.

This year (2020), my mom was placed in charge of the outreach department. It's her job to be the contact person for requests regarding grief that come in to the hospital from around the rest of America and the world. Right now, she's working with a hospital in Australia who has seen the transformative work at St. Jude and hopes to replicate it with a program of their own.

When the man who heads up the program gives presentations on the St. Jude Bereavement Program, he uses a slide that details the various points of impact through the program. In the center of it all is a photo of my brother Nick, because he believes that the grief that our family experienced ultimately led to the good work that has happened all over the world.

If that's true, then when cancer intended to harm us, God intended it for good to accomplish what is now being done, the saving of many lives. My brother's belief that God had an awesome plan through his life was not unfounded, because what has been accomplished is the saving of many lives.

In the last few months of his life, Nick learned how to play guitar and planned to start a band with a few of his friends. He envisioned that the name of the band would be The Positive Negatives, and while I'm not sure exactly what his thoughts were on the meaning, I can say that the name gives us a good picture of our darkest moments.

Perhaps there is redemption after all; a light of hope in the overwhelming grief of stories like Joseph and Naomi and Nick. Maybe, when it's all said and done and we look back on our lives, we'll see that they were the positive negatives.

PART IV

Defeat of Evil

CHAPTER NINE

To the Kingdom, Come

Does anyone remember the special ticketed event that featured Christian bands performing at various locations throughout Walt Disney World? The event was called Night of Joy, and from 1983 until 2017 anyone interested in hearing their favorite contemporary Christian music group could attend over the course of two evenings in September.

While the event is likely the nightmare fuel for many former and current Cast Members to this day (imagine working two nights where a park like Magic Kingdom gets primarily filled up by teenagers), it was a dream come true for a young adult youth pastor like me.

Night of Joy lasted for 35 years, but I was only able to attend three times. Living in Ohio, week-long concerts like the infamous Creation Festival were much easier to travel to—not to mention much cheaper to afford.

The tagline of the event was a play on words; a slightly altered version of the words found in The Lord's Prayer in Matthew 6:10. In the Scripture, the words of the prayer read "your kingdom come, your will be done on earth as it is in heaven." The tagline for Night of Joy was "To the Kingdom, come."

Do you get the double meaning intended? There's the obvious link to the prayer of Jesus, but the slight change allows room for the tagline to be a prayer of its own; an invitation for God (and Christians) to come to the Magic Kingdom for worship and community.

Like I said, there were portions of Night of Joy that were a little bit of sensory overload, specifically the deafening sound levels of screaming teenagers inside the queue for Space Mountain. May God have mercy on the poor Cast Members who worked the attraction those nights.

On the other hand, some of the most unique experiences I've ever had occurred during those evenings. While waiting in the line for Big Thunder Mountain Railroad, the entire crowd suddenly launched into a chorus of "How He Loves Us." Strangers stood together in front of the Pirates of the Caribbean stage and worshiped as one. And that's not to say anything of the Skillet concert on the Cinderella Castle stage that included fireworks and spinning sparklers fixed to the front of the Castle.

When I visit Walt Disney World, I'm constantly aware of multiple layers of meaning, purpose, and vision being impressed upon me. After a vacation filled with time spent inside the parks, I feel invigorated and re-energized to head back into my normal life with excitement. During the Night of Joy events, I could feel the additional layers that spending time with the community of fellow believers provided.

To borrow the lyric from Skillet's song off the *Comatose* album, "those nights kept me alive." I arrived at my first Night of Joy event burned out and frustrated over stressful situations that I was involved with at work, but as I flew home from Orlando I felt ready to conquer whatever lay ahead.

I mentioned to you in the introduction to this book that the place I feel closest to God is in a Florida swampland called Walt Disney World. There are many reasons for this, some of which we have already explored within the prior pages. I'll return to this again in chapter 12, when we wrap everything up. But for now, it's important that I note: I know that this feeling is partly not by accident—it's by design. I don't want to get the feeling of the "magic" mixed up with a true sense of God working in the world around me.

In other words, there are those who make the magic happen—intentionally, by design, every single day. Kingdoms are built purposefully and the Magic Kingdom is no different. It was constructed (originally in the form of Disneyland) to create an experience that produces a sense of joy, childlike wonder, and peace within you as you journey throughout it. And while a single parent with a screaming child in the middle of a 110 degree Frontierland may not agree, most of you can understand what I'm talking about when I mention the feeling of amazement that appears the moment you step past the gates.

All of this, of course, began with the vision from Walt Disney. In 1951, Walt worked alongside his friend Harper Goff (the man who had been put in charge as movie art director for all of the films that were produced by the Walt Disney Studios) on a completely new kind of project. The two of them started sketching out concepts for a theme park—something neither of them were familiar with in experience beforehand.

Walt pulled a handful of others into his dream: animators, writers, directors, and artists from his team who were skilled at creating scenes and bringing a story to life on the screen. While the animated and live action films continued to be produced, this group began to work behind the scenes to bring something *beyond* the movie screen to life.

One year later, the small team became officially known as WED (Walter Elias Disney) Enterprises—and later, simply "Imagineering". As the team designed the park that would ultimately open three years later in 1955, Walt gave them a directive:

> All I want you to think about is when people walk through or
> have access to anything you design, I want them, when they
> leave, to have smiles on their faces. Just remember that. It's
> all I ask of you as a designer.

That quote brings us back to what we were talking about just a moment ago. From the very beginning, a key purpose in the design of the parks was to create a feeling of happiness and to bring smiles to the faces of the guests. The process of making this happen involves the Imagineers' engagement of all of your senses as you walk through the park. Earlier, we talked about your visual sight and how it is tricked by forced perspective on Main Street. But what about our other four senses—taste, smell, touch, and sound?

I'm not sure I need to talk very much about how our sense of taste is engaged throughout the Disney Parks. From classics like Mickey bars and waffles to the Pineapple Dole Whip available in Adventureland, certain foods have been forever linked to our experience of Walt Disney World. It's not so much that the meatloaf, pot roast, and fried chicken entree at the 50s Prime Time Cafe is the absolute best meal I've ever had in my entire life...but when I'm eating it during dinner in Hollywood Studios, I pretty much believe it with my whole heart. That's not to say that there *aren't* some of the best foods in the world available at Walt Disney World, because there are. But let's be honest: Main Street popcorn is just a much more expensive version of the popcorn available in any store near us, and yes, we're still going to keep on buying it every time.

Your sense of smell is obviously activated via eating some of these classic foods, but that's only the beginning. Imagineers have placed machines called Smellitizers throughout the park, causing your nose to join into the stories that surround you. Outside Main Street Bakery, the smell of baked goods and candy is pumped out to the sidewalk. Near Pirates of the Caribbean, you can catch a whiff of sea water. At the Haunted Mansion, a familiar musty scent will engulf returning mortals. If you've ever been to EPCOT, you probably remember the citrusy smell of oranges while riding Soarin'. Some of the best parts of these attractions are the smells that accompany them.

All throughout the parks, guests are invited to reach out and touch everything around them. In the queue for Muppet Vision 3D, a sign notes "Back in 5 minutes—key is under mat." An adult might think little of this and continue moving towards the attraction, but a child or a child at heart can actually reach down, lift up the mat below the sign, and see the real key on the floor.

A few streets over, outside the Indiana Jones Epic Stunt Spectacular, you can spot a well with a rope going down inside of it. Next to the well is a sign that states "WARNING: DO NOT PULL ROPE." This has deterred many law-abiding guests from going further, but a closer look will reveal that the "not" on the sign has been crossed out—and so pulling on the rope is exactly what you're meant to do.

Your ears are constantly taking in all sorts of sounds while you're on Disney property. Each area you enter has either background music that sets the tone, or alternatively, sounds of the local nature (like you'll notice in Pandora, the world of Avatar). Many of the attractions include musical themes or songs, most of them that will likely get stuck in your head and resurface later. As I write this, It's a Small World is playing via Sorcerer Radio...do I need to say any more?

All five of your senses are being engaged, on purpose and with planned intent, so that when you leave at the end of the day you will ultimately have a smile on your face, just as Walt said. Every Disney Kingdom—from Animal Kingdom to Tokyo DisneySea and Disneyland Paris—is built with this end in mind, and the Imagineers achieve their goal every single day across the globe.

When it comes to addressing the problem of evil, pain, and sadness in the world, Walt Disney has done his part to combat the darkness by introducing a bit of hope and peace through his various Kingdoms...but I'll never forget reading about what happened at Walt Disney World on September 11, 2001.

It was, of course, the day of the terrorist attacks on the World Trade Center in New York City. While the day started as any other day might at the happiest place on earth, it soon became clear that this would in fact be an unprecedented moment in the history of not only the Walt Disney Company, but the entire world.

There are many heartbreaking stories of those receiving the news of the attacks, but the tales of the Magic Kingdom on that day stand out. Because the normal feeling in the parks is the happiness we've just discussed, September 11th stands in stark contrast to anything ever experienced on the property before or after.

An average guest walking around the parks that day had very little to no knowledge about the events unfolding in New York. Keep in mind that 2001 was before smart phones (and even texting) became popular, so no one was carrying around constant updates in their pocket. Additionally, when the first tower was hit, people everywhere across the nation began calling their loved ones—which overloaded the system and rendered most outgoing calls ineffective. There are no TVs within the parks that show the news or other channels, so information was limited to whatever the Cast Members were willing to share.

On that terrible day, executives of the Parks division of the Walt Disney Company made the hard but necessary decision to close all of their parks worldwide for the rest of the day. Because Walt Disney World is such a huge crowd drawing place, it's safe to say that both executives and the United States government were concerned about the potential of another attack being aimed at the parks.

To prevent the inciting of panicked crowds within the parks, a simple yet effective message played over all loudspeakers, in every land and on every attraction: "Due to circumstances beyond our control, the Magic Kingdom is now closed. Please follow the direction of the nearest Cast Member."

Cast Members did not give further explanation to the closing, but instead joined hands across lands and slowly walked towards the central Hub in front of Cinderella Castle, ensuring that guests would be moved towards and down Main Street, USA. From there, they would be directed to the exit where they could get a bus to their resort hotel or catch a monorail back to their car at the Transportation and Ticketing Center to head home, where they could safely learn the news themselves.

One guest who stayed at Disney's Yacht Club watched as a military gunship flew "overhead so closely that my wife could clearly see someone manning one of the machine guns." This was certainly not a sight that had ever been seen in the sky above Walt Disney World before.

As hard as Walt Disney and the Imagineers worked in building of their Kingdom, and as hard as Cast Members work every single day to maintain the magic and preserve the happiness and smiles, darkness still managed to invade the Kingdom. The animators and storytellers may have been able to come up with a solution for the problem of Maleficent in Fantasmic, but there was no way they could have planned for or concocted a solution to the real life evil that appeared on that day.

All throughout history, humans have offered up solutions to combat the problems, darkness, and evil that we see all around us. Ultimately, we hope that we could see the defeat of evil, and that in that moment we would experience nothing but peace and prosperity, a time in which we would no longer need to fear the possibility of any dark surprises like September 11th again.

Strangely, as people have grappled with the means by which to achieve this possible worldwide peace, we have adopted all sorts of methods that seem to be the exact opposite of the harmony we're hoping to attain. There are many examples of this, but for our purposes it might be most helpful to consider the Roman Empire within the 1st century AD, within the lifetime of Jesus.

It's no secret to anyone who has taken a world history class that Rome dominated the ancient world. No matter where you found yourself in during the first century, you would be sure to find the fingerprints of the Romans. For about a two hundred year period, from 27 BC to 180 AD, Rome actually achieved a peace throughout all of its territories which they called the Pax Romana (the peace of Rome).

As we consider that short period of peace in history, we have to first think about what it took to get to that point. In order for Rome to rule and establish their peace, their military marched across the various lands and violently conquered country after county, submitting the people to their will or to the sword.

So to establish peace, we first must enact countless acts of violence? According to the Roman Empire (and the Galactic Empire, for that matter), that's exactly what we need to do.

It wasn't just outsiders and people from other nations who became victims of the warpath. Conduct a quick search on Google for Roman civil wars, and you'll find a seemingly endless list of fights between leaders within their own nation. Everyone wanted a slice of power for themselves—they wanted to be the ones to personally usher in the peace of Rome—and many of them were willing to kill to make their dream come true.

One of the most famous of the civil wars was actually the last, the tragic story of a series of battles between Octavian and Marc Antony. In the Republic Senate, Octavian made a strong case for enacting war against the Egyptian Queen, Cleopatra. The problem for Antony was that Cleopatra was actually his lover—so of course he was set against any action being taken that would negatively harm her nation.

While Marc Antony did receive some support from others within the Senate, he was in the minority. When his people and their armies rose up against Octavian and his armies, Antony found himself on the run. Eventually, he and Cleopatra tried to hide within the Egyptian city of Alexandra, but Octavian found them there and continued to besiege the city until the two of them committed suicide in desperation.

With his enemy out of the way, Octavian returned to the Republic Senate, who voted that he would become the first Emperor of Rome. Shortly afterwards, it was announced that the Republic of Rome was no more—instead, Octavian would reroute all decision making power to himself in the newly formed "Roman Empire". (It seems clear where George Lucas got his inspiration for Palpatine taking power from the Senate in *Revenge of the Sith*, doesn't it?)

In order to reach the tranquility of the Pax Romana, Romans and outsiders alike had to die. The problems with this thinking are somewhat evident, because they seem to counteract the very peace we are trying to bring. If we can experience peace for 200 years, yet that peace comes at the cost of many lives to achieve it, is it actually worthwhile?

Depending on the kind of peace we're talking about, you might be inclined to say that it *is* worth it—but let's think about the version of serenity that Rome's Kingdom brought to the citizens under its control.

When Jesus was very young, history tells us that a small rebel force in Israel was empowered when a local Roman ruler, King Herod, died. They attempted to rise up and gain control of their homeland, but were quickly snuffed out by the troops. To make an example of these rebels, the Roman General Quintilius Varus decided to crucify 2,000 of them on the road leading to Jerusalem. It would be impossible to miss for anyone heading down this well traveled road, and the message was even more obvious: if you stand against Rome, death instead of peace is what you will end up with.

There are countless examples of this playing out again and again throughout that 200 year period, but it just goes to show that the supposed Pax Romana was not true peace after all—it was only extended to those who supported the Emperor, and it still involved vast amounts of death, torture, and injustice.

When humans attempt to bring peace to the world, we consistently seem to screw it up because we just can't seem to envision a way to do it without first conquering someone, putting others under our control, or fighting our way to the top. Human Kingdoms are full of these kind of opposing and confusing ideals, and if we're looking forward to the defeat of evil, it doesn't seem likely that we'll achieve it through Kingdoms of violence.

All of this reminds me of a famous passage in the Gospels, the one where Jesus rides into Jerusalem on a donkey (often referred to as Palm Sunday). After the famous ride, where people shouted "peace in heaven and glory in the highest," the Gospel of Luke tells us that Jesus wept over the city because they had a completely wrong viewpoint on where that peace could come from:

> If you, even you, had only known on this day what would bring you peace—but now it is hidden from your eyes. The days will come upon you when your enemies will build an embankment against you and encircle you and hem you in on every side. They will dash you to the ground, you and the children within your walls. They will not leave one stone on another, because you did not recognize the time of God's coming to you.
> —Luke 19:42-44

The people on that day *had* recognized Jesus as their King, saying "blessed is the king who comes in the name of the Lord!" But sadly, their version of a King was one who would rise up in violent rebellion to destroy Rome—and that's exactly who they thought Jesus would become. They assumed their version of peace was about to be enacted through an uprising, but Jesus cried in the knowledge that true peace can never be found that way. He envisioned a grisly scene for those in Jerusalem who continued to follow their own wisdom about how to defeat the evil around them.

Almost forty years later, in 70 AD, the vision of Jesus came to pass. Still looking for a chance to follow a leader who could lead a Jewish army against the Roman Empire, zealous citizens rose up and advanced against Rome...only to be crushed, defeated, and destroyed. Jewish historian Josephus was present during the bloody event, and shares what he saw after a Roman soldier threw a burning torch into the temple in Jerusalem in his book *The Jewish War*:

> As the flames shot up, the Jews let out a shout of dismay that matched the tragedy; they flocked to the rescue with no thought of sparing their lives or husbanding their strength; for the sacred structure they had guarded with such devotion was vanishing before their eyes.
>
> Most of the slain were peaceful citizens, weak and unarmed, and they were butchered where they were caught. The heap of corpses mounted higher and higher about the altar; a stream of blood flowed down the Temple's steps, and bodies of those slain slipped from the top to the bottom.
>
> The Temple Mount, everywhere enveloped in flames, seemed to be boiling over from its base; yet the blood seemed more abundant than the flames and the numbers of the slain greater than those of the slayers. The soldiers climbed over heaps of bodies as they chased the fugitives.

Just like the Romans, the Jewish people found out what happens when you decide to pursue peace via the sword—you end up dying by the sword. But hadn't Jesus alluded to something that actually *could* bring peace back in the Luke passage? By saying "if you had only known on this day what would bring you peace," doesn't that clearly infer that there is something to be known, a true peace that can be obtained; a final and lasting defeat of evil? Could there be a Kingdom established that won't fail to provide true prosperity and tranquility?

The answer of the Scriptures is clearly yes, but it's not accessible in any of the logical violent ways of conquering that we often come up with. Instead, the Scriptures maintain that Jesus became King over the universe and defeated evil through his death on a Roman execution device, the cross. It's a counterintuitive idea that doesn't even register for most of us—to consider that evil could be defeated by dying makes little sense.

But aren't even our favorite stories filled with this kind of self-sacrificial love? The Beast, Rapunzel, Obi-Wan Kenobi, Tony Stark, Raymond the firefly, the list goes on... all of them willing to die for the sake of those they love.

In the case of Jesus though, we don't even see a battle where he fights with the Romans and then ultimately is willing to be killed. He willingly and knowingly goes to the cross, forgiving those who put him there with the full belief that it is the very act of his death that will cause the ultimate defeat of evil.

Paul talks about the seeming foolishness of this plan in 1 Corinthians 1:

> For the message of the cross is foolishness to those who are perishing, but to us who are being saved it is the power of God...we preach Christ crucified: a stumbling block to the Jews and foolishness to the Gentiles, but to those whom God has called, both Jews and Greeks, Christ the power of God and the wisdom of God...God chose the foolish things of the world to shame the wise; God chose the weak things of the world to shame the strong.
>
> —1 Corinthians 1:18,23,27

How did God choose to establish His Kingdom that would never fall? He died as the ultimate act of love, was resurrected on the third day, and in that moment had the victory over the powers of evil and darkness. Later on, Paul puts it this way:

> Death has been swallowed up in victory. Where, O death, is your victory? Where, O death, is your sting? The sting of death is sin, and the power of sin is the law. But thanks be to God! He gives us the victory through our Lord Jesus Christ.
> — 1 Corinthians 15:54-57

Conflict comes to us all in this life, and death will eventually happen to each and every one of us...but death and darkness no longer have the last word. In the darkest times like that fateful day of the terrorist attack in 2001, we can still have viable hope and peace knowing that love has already won the war.

The victory is already won—and now, we're all invited to live in the midst of that reality and that Kingdom in the present.

To the Kingdom, come.

CHAPTER TEN

The Destiny of a Jedi

As you continue to navigate through all of the adventures and quests that God reveals to you, one of your most important tasks will be to keep reminding yourself of the victory we just discussed in the last chapter. As we face the inevitable conflict in each of the stories we take part in, it can become increasingly hard to press on towards our goal.

Many people have given up on their God-given adventure because they felt as if the odds mounting against them were too large to overcome. It is true that there are times and situations in which you might realize God is leading you in a different direction than you originally envisioned, but we can't use that as an excuse to just give up when things get difficult.

I'm reminded of the founder of my specific church tradition, the Free Methodist Church. In 1858, Benjamin Titus Roberts (B.T. for short) was expelled as a minister in the Methodist Episcopal Church. What was one of his greatest crimes that led to this result?

Well, in a time when slavery was still legal in America, B.T. was very outspoken against enslavement, calling all Christians to support abolitionism. Sadly, the leadership of the time in the Methodist Episcopal Church did not want to stand on either side, opting instead of stay silent on issues of freedom and slavery. B.T. Roberts called out the fear of his own denomination, publishing a public pamphlet that denounced them for not supporting freedom for all people.

Once he was expelled from the MEC, he founded the Free Methodist Church—a group that would stand as abolitionists, regardless of who thought they were wrong.

What if B.T. would have given into the same fear that seemed to dominate many in that age who stayed silent? What if he had faced all of the conflict from his denomination and decided "well, they're in charge, and if they are so against me being an abolitionist, then I guess God is leading me in a different direction."

B.T. didn't blink in the face of adversity because he knew he was aligned with God's adventure—ending slavery and providing freedom for all people. When you're certain about His call, you don't need to spend restless nights tossing and turning about if you've missed the boat. You can be certain of victory, the defeat of evil and the overcoming of any conflict, when you know without a doubt you're aligned with God's plan. The words of Romans 8:31 will be found true in your life:

If God is for us, who can be against us?

Even in the midst of this knowledge, it can be hard to accept the reality of the Kingdom we talked about. It's one thing to quote Bible verses and to claim that Jesus has already become King over all the universe through his death and resurrection—but it's another thing entirely to try to put that into practice.

In the midst of the hardships we see all around us and personally face each day, how could it all be true? How could darkness actually be defeated by Christ, considering that we all could give countless examples of evil in our current world. Even if it is all true, how could we keep the victory of the light in the forefront of our minds as we move throughout our own God-given adventures?

To put all of that another way: how do we see this defeat of evil with the eyes of the Kingdom?

For many Christians, the problem is not that we completely disbelieve the message of the Scripture. Instead, it has become a matter of listening to either the voice of fear or the voice of love. When we listen to our fears, which come from and are supplied by the powers of darkness, we often end up stumbling in confusion and anxiety... but when we listen to the voice of love (which is supplied by Christ), we flourish and see things as they truly are. When we listen to and are guided by the voice of love, we see through the eyes of the Kingdom.

Interestingly, the Bible pits these two against each other. Although we might guess that the opposite of love is hate, time and time again it seems as if the authors of the Scriptures place *fear* on the opposite side of the spectrum to love. Fear seems to animate many (if not all) of the other problems like anger, hate and regret.

When it comes to our adventure, what is one of the biggest fears we can expect to encounter? Here's a hint: we talked about it in chapter 7...it's failure. Often, we judge our value and the importance of what we're doing based upon the response. If we don't get a big reaction or a bunch of people applauding us for what we're doing, we think we've failed and that it wasn't worth our time.

This could have happened to Walt many different times throughout his life, as we've already illustrated with the making of *Snow White* and the opening day of Disneyland. For Walt though, the failures weren't limited to just those who responded by calling his work a "folly."

On the wall of my home office hangs a painting of a rabbit. He doesn't wear a shirt, only gray shorts, and most of his body from his long ears to his hands and feet are dark black. Only his face is white, and if you were to study it for a moment you might find yourself wondering he looks so familiar.

Perhaps you've already guessed—the rabbit I'm talking about is actually Oswald the Lucky Rabbit, and the reason you recognize his face is because it looks almost identical to Mickey Mouse. If you've never heard of Oswald, I'm only slightly surprised. The majority of his story took place between 1927 and 1938, and until 2006 the character had all but disappeared from the planet.

For a time, it seemed as if Oswald the Lucky Rabbit might have been the character face of the Disney Company far into the future. Instead of the Partners statue of Walt holding hands with Mickey in front of Cinderella Castle, we almost were presented with a version of history where Oswald replaced Mickey in that prominent place.

In an era where cartoon characters existed simply as a means to deliver gags, Oswald was created by Walt and his friend Ub Iwerks as the first character to actually have a personality. He wasn't just another cat animation (commonly used at the time) who got hit on the head with anvils for a cheap laugh. There was something special about Oswald that set him apart from all of the other characters out there.

Unfortunately, a man named Charles Mintz tricked Walt into giving away the rights to Oswald to Universal Pictures. (Mintz is the real life inspiration behind Charles Muntz, the villain in *Up*. There's only one letter of difference in their names!) In a day, not only had Walt lost Oswald—he had also lost half of his animation team, who were stolen away by Mintz with an alluring deal.

Only a week later after receiving this devastating news, Walt drew Mickey Mouse for the first time, who turned out to be an even bigger success than Oswald had been. In fact, it was Mintz who ultimately failed as he attempted to use his stolen character to no avail. The world was now in love with Mickey, and Walt could rightly say later that "it all started with a mouse."

It's interesting to consider the kinds of thoughts that may have passed through Walt Disney's head within the week after Oswald was taken. At the most extreme, perhaps he thought that his adventure was at an end...but at the very least, he must have seen the loss of Oswald as a massive failure. Little did he know at the time that Mickey was right around the corner.

Speaking of failure, do you remember what Yoda said to Luke in *The Last Jedi*? After Luke attempts to train Ben Solo and it ends in chaos through Ben's turning to the dark side, he falls apart and spends years sitting in the mess of his perceived failure. Gone is the strong Jedi Master we once knew from *Return of the Jedi*, replaced with almost a parody of Luke himself. He has no strength to speak of, no lightsaber, no courage—he just sits around in self-inflicted quarantine in his huts while he watches the porgs fly around his little island.

The force ghost of Yoda appears, burning up the sacred Jedi texts. After a brief conversation, Yoda guides Luke back to what is truly important and reveals in his unique way:

> Heeded my words not, did you? Pass on what you have learned. Strength. Mastery. But weakness, folly, failure also. Yes, failure most of all. The greatest teacher, failure is.

What if we could bring ourselves to believe the same thing? What if we looked at failure and could come to believe that it was actually going to lead us into an even greater understanding of our world; a refined and better knowledge of our quest?

If we could do that, could we even viably call it a failure at all? If we ultimately ended up learning more and becoming better because of it, was it a defeat or actually a victory? Could we call the debacle with Oswald a failure in the full knowledge that Mickey would have likely never existed?

All of this leads us back to where we were a few moments ago, thinking about seeing through the eyes of the Kingdom and love instead of listening to the whispers of fear. The truth is, the only version of reality that matters (and thus, the only version that is actually real) is the one that God defines and sets forth. Anything else that comes in opposition, that which comes from the mouth of fear, is an illusion.

This is not to say that the bad things are somehow not real or that evil does not exist; instead it is to say that in the light of the reality of the Kingship of Christ, evil and darkness have absolutely no power, and any power we thought they may have had in the world is nothing but an illusion. The fate and destruction of evil has already been sealed and won on the cross.

Even though we are not yet living in that perfect reality where there are no more tears, pain, or darkness, those who place their trust in Christ already have citizenship in that Kingdom. We are merely refugees in this place of darkness, and we live according to different standards. Our eyes should be open to the realities of the Kingdom of which we are citizens, which should then in turn affect our response and reactions to the darkness of this world. This is what Peter had in mind when he wrote:

> I urge you, as aliens and strangers in the world, to abstain from sinful desires, which war against your soul. Live such good lives among the pagans that, though they accuse you of doing wrong, they may see your good deeds and glorify God on the day he visits us.
> —1 Peter 2:11-12

This was written in a day when "pagans" referred to people like the Romans, who were known for torturing Christians and killing them in gruesome ways. Even in the face of impending death, followers of Jesus were encouraged to look through the lens of the Kingdom. James, the brother of Jesus, follows this line of thinking later on:

> Consider it pure joy, my brothers, whenever you face trials of many kinds, because you know that the testing of your faith develops perseverance.
> —James 1:2-3

Paul, across the letters he writes to different churches, says things like: "we rejoice in our sufferings," (Romans

5:3) and "I consider that the sufferings of this present time are not worth comparing with the glory that is revealed to us." (Romans 8:18) One of the clearest passages he writes on the subject reveals that

> Our light and momentary troubles are achieving for us an eternal glory that far outweighs them all. So we fix our eyes not on what is seen, but on what is unseen. For what is seen is temporary, but what is unseen is eternal.
> —2 Corinthians 4:17-18)

How could any of these authors in the early church claim that facing the darkness of torture was to be considered "pure joy?" Why would anyone in their right minds refer to the potential of impending death as "light and momentary troubles?"

Depending on your point of view, it's entirely possible—if you're looking through the right lens, the glasses of the Kingdom of God. Regardless of what someone may do to your physical body with threat or sword, those in Christ are promised the hope of resurrection...and thus no one can truly touch you.

In the words of Obi-Wan Kenobi while facing Darth Vader in *A New Hope*: "You can't win, Darth. If you strike me down, I shall become more powerful than you could possibly imagine."

Yes, it's a fictional sci-fi movie set in a galaxy far, far away. But if the hope of the resurrection of Jesus is true, then those who die in Christ are resurrected to a life after this one that greatly surpasses anything we could have hoped for on this earth. In that knowledge, your soul (your true self) is untouchable and your body is simply a sort of "costume" that will one day fade away.

The darkness has already lost the war, evil has already been defeated, and death no longer has any sting. The light shines in the darkness, and the darkness has not overcome it (John 1:5).

From the wide scope of the fullness of your life to the daily decisions needed to advance your God-given adventures in this world, we must keep the perspective of the Kingdom at the forefront of our minds each and every day. If we can achieve this, we'll find ourselves thriving with boldness, strength, and wisdom as we courageously jump into all the sorts of adventures God reveals to us along the way.

The enemy of this rich kind of life is fear, because fear is the antithesis of the Kingdom of love. Fear will do anything it can to derail you, to stop your progress in your quest, or to try to convince you that you can't do whatever it is that God has called you to do.

How do we fight this invisible enemy and defeat the villain that has haunted so many of us? It's simple: we live in love. If living in fear keeps us from seeing the Kingdom, it only makes sense that living moment to moment in the Kingdom will keep fear at bay. John writes about this in one of his letters:

> God is love. Whoever lives in love lives in God, and God in him. In this way, love is made complete among us so that we will have confidence on the day of judgment, because in this world we are like him. There is no fear in love. But perfect love drives out fear, because fear has to do with punishment. The one who fears is not made perfect in love.
> —1 John 4:16-17

As apprentices of Jesus, we're nowhere close to being a protector of a galaxy far, far away. But our goal as followers of him is very well summarized in the line from Luke to Rey in *The Rise of Skywalker* when he notes, "Confronting fear is the destiny of a Jedi."

We must be willing and ready to confront our fear each and every day in order to be "made perfect in love." How do we live in love and the truth? In this case, the standard "Sunday school" answer is actually correct: we spend time with God in prayer, submit ourselves to a reading (and then applying to our lives) of Scripture, and involve ourselves in a church where we can be surrounded with fellow believers.

As a pastor that has spent my life attending church services, youth groups, and even church staff meetings, I'm willing to admit that the answer I've just provided may seem a little like a letdown. Much of the time, prayer can seem like the boring choice when alternatively we could get started with some sort of action steps right away. Similarly, for those of us who have had access to Bibles our entire lives, reading the Bible can seem somewhat stale. It's easy to claim we're going to start attending church as a New Year's Resolution, but when the second Sunday of January rolls around we get busy watching *The Imagineering Story* on Disney+, and by the time we've finished the series we have already gotten out of the rhythm.

Yet regardless of how we may sometimes feel, we must understand that these are the three main tools we've been given in our earthly battle against the enemy of fear. Prayer was never meant to be a stale or boring time that makes us fall asleep, but instead the very means by which we might access the insight, power, and wisdom of God. This is the example Jesus gives in the Gospels—he is constantly spending time away on his own in order to preform ministry.

Like Jesus while being tempted in the desert, we can fight the lies that fear presents to us by knowing and living by Scripture, because it reveals to us the truth of the Kingdom—the words and reality from God himself (Matthew 4:1-11). Being a part of a healthy church allows us to consistently realize that we are not traveling through this life alone—and that we all need each other with all of our individual strengths to succeed (1 Corinthians 12:1-11).

If we are missing any one of these vital elements, we will find ourselves forgetting the reality of the Kingdom and instead stumbling in the darkness of fear. I know a great family of strong Christians who spend time in prayer and reading of the Bible, but they don't place much importance in gathering together consistently with other believers. As a result, they're missing out on the fullness of life that God has made available to them. This was the point the author of Hebrews was attempting to make when they said:

> Let us consider how we may spur one another on toward love and good deeds. Let us not give up meeting together, as some are in the habit of doing, but let us encourage one another— and all the more as you see the Day approaching.
>
> —Hebrews 10:24-25

Use all of the tools made available to you to align your eyes with the Kingdom. While we will still encounter sadness, conflict, and pain within this earth, we yearn and look for the Day when everything is renewed once and for all. In the meantime, we head towards the excitement of our climactic scenes...

PART V

The New Life Begins

CHAPTER ELEVEN

Dreams Come True

Maybe you've already started to get an idea of what adventure God is asking you to be a part of, or maybe you are still thinking about how to best use your strengths to do something meaningful in the world. Perhaps you've known for a very long time what you need to do next, but you just haven't taken the next step like you should.

Whichever stage you find yourself in, you can be certain that as you finally embark there is one key piece of the journey you'll need to keep at the forefront of your mind: the climactic scene. Think way back to the first chapter and what we discussed: the climactic scene happens at the end of the story when all of the struggles have been overcome, like all of the servants and the Prince becoming human again with Gaston completely out of the picture.

If God is currently leading you into the next chapter of your life that involves going to college and taking classes, then your climactic scene could be the image of walking across the stage to receive your diploma while friends and family clap excitedly. If you've felt it's time to start spending more focused time investing in your coworkers, then it might be a vision of a team of people who not only work together, but truly love each other and look out for one another.

Whatever ending you're hoping to see come to fruition, purposefully remind yourself of it again and again and again. The potential excitement of achieving your triumph will fuel you with the energy you need to keep moving towards meaningful things, instead of getting sidetracked halfway through the conflict and deciding to return to watching TV on the couch. You're not only *able* to achieve your God-given dreams—you will also be *eager* to achieve that ending and thus *willing* to travel the distance in between the starting line and that achievement.

Walt Disney certainly had this process down to a science. He had the uncanny ability to envision his dreams in his mind and then not only transfer those images to paper in drawings, but to actually overcome all of the hurdles necessary to make all of those dreams come true.

One of Walt's most famous quotes, often printed on walls that conceal portions of Disney property that are under construction, claims that "All of our dreams can come true, if we have the courage to pursue them."

It's the kind of thing we would expect someone to say if they spend their life working with characters like Jiminy Cricket and the Fairy Godmother from *Cinderella.* "Dreams come true" is a phrase repeated not only in the vast catalog of Disney films, but every day in a wide array of situations around Walt Disney World. We might write it off to some extent, thinking that it's a nice sounding phrase but unsure of just how true it actually could be.

It might be easy for you to come up with a climactic scene, but there's a huge difference between coming up with a dream in your head and actually making it happen in the real world, beyond your imagination. Despite this truth, I believe that all of your dreams *can* actually become a reality if they are truly coming from God and you are willing to courageously pursue them.

Does your personal climactic scene involve loving God and loving people in some sort of way? Then you're probably on the right track for an important quest! If your scene is all about you driving off a car lot with a brand new Porsche, then it's probably time to go back to the drawing board, because you're going to figure out sooner than later that you're living out one of those boring stories again.

Don't get me wrong—there's nothing wrong with buying a needed car. It's just that our life needs to be about something bigger than ourselves and our physical possessions if we hope to find long lasting meaning. Dreams that focus on furthering the love of God or the love of other people will accomplish the kind of meaning we're looking for.

Walt's dream of Disneyland honed in on his love for people, especially families. When he realized that he was consistently separated from his daughters on their weekly "Daddy's Day," given that he would sit on a bench eating peanuts and the girls would ride the merry-go-round, he began to dream even more about the possibility of a place where "parents and children could have fun together."

You may have had the pleasure of walking down Main Street, U.S.A., but can you imagine what it must have felt like to be Walt Disney walking down that street at Disneyland for the very first time when it was in the midst of being built? What must he have felt when the entire park was complete, and he could walk throughout it from land to land? When guests began to fill the streets and board the attractions, what were some of Walt's thoughts as he actually saw parents and children having fun together before his very eyes?

Whatever he felt and experienced, we can be sure it was exhilarating, because witnessing the fruition of your hard work and struggle play out into success is the best part of the entire journey.

It's possible that you might change some of your plans along the way. I've met many people, for example, who imagined a goal of finishing college as being their next step towards their calling. Even though that was a noble quest and seemed to be the next correct step, some of them found while taking their classes that there was actually a better path besides college that could help them achieve their desired job. After dropping out of college and abandoning that earlier envisioned scene of graduation, they found an even better option that presented them with a new climax to their present story.

I'm not sure if I should mention this, because I'm absolutely *not* attempting to convince teenagers to drop out of high school, but...did you know that Walt himself never graduated high school (and thus never attended any college either)?

It's true. At age 16, he dropped out of high school in hopes that he might join the army to fight in World War I. At first, it looked like his dream of helping his country was a complete mistake as he was rejected as a recruit for being too young. But in his normal persistence, he looked for and found a loophole—and was soon employed as an ambulance driver with the Red Cross, assisting those who were injured while fighting for America.

Again, my point isn't to inspire any teenagers reading this to rip up your textbooks and storm out of the school with a determined grin, because I don't think your parents would be very appreciative of that kind of a dream. But I do want to make clear that your goal may change along the way, and that's okay. Don't grasp too tightly onto your climactic scene that you become unwilling to be open to change.

Part of a good journey is often realizing that the trail is leading down a slightly different path than you first thought it would when you charted things out. That doesn't mean that you were totally confused or mislead when you thought that God was calling you to a certain adventure. If you think carefully, what you'll often find is that you would never have gotten to the place you are *now* unless you had gone through those very steps on the first trail.

It seems to me that very often, God doesn't give us all of the details—he just asks us to start on the journey.

A great example of this is found within the story of Abraham, where God asked him to leave what was comfortable to him for an uncharted land:

> Leave your country, your people and your father's household, and go to the land I will show you.
> —Genesis 12:1

Abraham was the original Elsa, heading into the unknown with no real knowledge of where he was heading or what he might do once he arrived. This was in a day where kids didn't move away from their parents when they grew up...instead, they would just build their own wing onto their father's household.

So here's Abraham being asked to leave what is customary, normal, and familiar to him for a land that God will "show him." If I were Abraham, I would have liked to have at least a little more information about where I was headed. Is it Disneyland Paris? Can that be the land you're showing me or...? It's at least not going to be bad, right?

Abraham doesn't get any clues about the land that God will show him before he makes the choice to head out the door, but he does get a glimpse of the climactic scene for his life. If he chooses to follow God's command, he is promised by God:

> I will make you into a great nation and I will bless you; I will make your name great, and you will be a blessing. I will bless those who bless you, and whoever curses you I will curse; and all peoples on earth will be blessed through you.
> —Genesis 12:2-3

He still doesn't know specifically where he's going, but he's aware of this promise that if he is willing to head to this yet to be named place, he's going to end up as "a great nation." Fast forward all these years later, and we get to see what that line was all about—history tells us that Abraham was the "father" of the nation of Israel. He gave up all of those familiar aspects of his life, but he traded them in for something bigger and better when it was all said and done.

Last year, I felt that God might be calling me into an adventure of helping to end modern-day slavery. The biggest problem with this calling was that I didn't know much about modern-day slavery (often called human trafficking), which seemed like a big deficiency. Not only was I unsure about how to address the problem, but I was also not quite sure if I could make a tangible difference.

Fast forward to the present, and I'm working with a small team of people in our local area who are directly reaching those who are affected by trafficking. This past month, we heard from a woman in our area who literally has a house that she's hoping to turn into a safe drop-in center for our victims.

Our team only knew we were headed in the direction of freedom, but now we're consistently seeing transformation and doors opening in all sorts of new ways that expand the vision of the dream I had over a year ago.

Keep the finish line of your dream at the very front of your mind, because it will help you to move forward with courage. If that finish line changes, that's okay too because in the midst of what we call the unknown, God clearly recognizes as the known to Him. He has our future in His hands, and at times we get to be surprised by the twists and turns in the story.

The most important advice for success is simple, and can be summarized by yet another quote from Walt: "The difference between winning and losing is often not quitting."

You want to be successful at living a meaningful story and fulfilling your God-given dreams? The best thing you can do is simply *not* quit.

In the meantime, there's a climactic scene that has been promised in the Scriptures, and it's one that speaks to the very depth of our souls...

CHAPTER TWELVE

Like Mist and Water

This past summer, my neighbor Ron died. Even though he was in his seventies, it was still unexpected for everyone who knew him. He had all sorts of daily aches and pains after years of teaching karate classes, but he didn't allow that to stop him from getting up every morning and mowing someone else's grass or dancing on his porch to the music he blasted from his radio.

Ron was a strong Christian who allowed his faith to influence the outlook on his daily life, and when he died the entire neighborhood felt his absence. I remember going for a run when I heard the news, then sitting in my front yard for a bit—looking across the street to where he lived and listening to songs that came through my headphones. The lyrics to one tune began to stand out from a band called The Gray Havens ("Forever," on the album *She Waits*):

> So here we go, like mist and water that's here and gone. But here we'll stay, on forever—be back someday. 'Cause forever is in my soul, it's in my veins, and it won't let go.

In the middle of the tragedy of unexpected death, the ultimate hope was reflected in the fact that our lives on this earth are like mist and water. In the bigger picture of things, our life is like a vapor that is here one minute and gone the next, but that is not the end of the story.

Over the course of these last eleven chapters, we've talked about your personal journey on a small and large scale. Of course, each of our adventures will likely look different from each other—I felt that my latest adventure was to write this book, while you might find yourself being asked to consider the adoption process, to invite a neighbor over to your house for a meal, or to run (and complete) your very first marathon. If it's to run and complete your very first mile, then that's great too!

I won't assume that you, the reader, are necessarily a follower of Jesus. We may not yet have that in common (although I hope you have potentially given it more consideration during our time together). If you have gotten to this point in the book, it seems to me that despite all of the potential differences that may be present in our individual lives, we have at least two things in common: a love for all things Disney, and the hope that we might make something of our lives so that we did not live without purpose.

Some of my absolute favorite memories at Walt Disney World have happened late at night during extended trips that afforded me the time to purposefully slow down. With seven days worth of tickets to the parks, I no longer feel as if I need to rush for anything. At midnight, I'm willing to stand in the surprisingly (still) long line at Main Street Bakery to wait for an iced latte without feeling like I have to run towards Space Mountain.

On these types of nights, I'll head with my coffee to the Hub and sit down on one of the benches. After a long sip of the Chestnut Praline Latte that's available during the Christmas season, I'll close my eyes for a moment and take a deliberate deep breath through my nose, attempting to catch all of the smells around me in addition to the warm and fresh Florida night air.

I resist any urge to be distracted by the notifications on my phone or even the temptation to take it out and snap some photos. There has been time for that, and there will be more time for all of that later. In that moment, looking from Main Street to the neon of Tomorrowland and then back towards the Castle, I am inspired and reinvigorated and fueled by much more than the caffeine in my drink. I am ready to head home after my vacation and live purposefully like Walt did; to dream impossible dreams and to make them become reality with the help of God.

And then, before I decide to leave the bench, I'm eventually reminded of the words to a song I played over and over and over again growing up. It was on a cassette tape called *Music From the Park*, an album that collected all sorts of famous artists from the time singing various Disney songs. The final track is called "Remember the Magic," and it features these lyrics sung by Brian McKnight:

> Can you remember back to a simpler time? Back to the water-color days that still run through your mind...Oh, I remember just my old friend and me runnin' through an open field, the way it used to be—the feeling that our hearts would just take wings, we could live a world of dreams; together we could sail against the wind.

Thinking though those lyrics (especially during those reflective moments inside the park) is nostalgic in a way that contains notes of sadness. Because although in that moment I am experiencing the perfection of the spellbinding sights and smells of the Magic Kingdom, I will soon find myself back in the "real world."

And as inspired as I am to keep moving forward in my adventure in my normal life, there's a part of me that longs to keep the perfection of what I'm being presented with in that moment on the bench. It reminds me of a simpler time when I was younger, where my summer days were spent literally exploring in open fields with my friend Zach, just like the song by Brian McKnight.

In those days, I wasn't yet aware of all the conflict in the world. In my early years, I didn't have to deal with tragedies like my neighbor Ron dying, because for a short few years in my childhood there was just a simple sense of things being at perfect peace. Even though I'm simultaneously aware that Cinderella Castle is still a facade and the Smellitizer is pumping out that aroma of cookies I'm smelling, sitting on that bench still produces—just for a moment—that feeling of everything being right in the world.

I wouldn't trade life with my two daughters and wife for anything, so I'm not spending those minutes wishing for some other life or that I could go back in time to perpetually be a child. Instead, I yearn for a kind of place and life where we no longer have to deal with reports of racial injustice, murder, or hurricanes.

No matter who you are, I think that possibly one of the biggest reasons you love Walt Disney World so much is that it reflects the kind of Kingdom we all yearn for; a peaceable Kingdom of love and hope that we experience in part now but not in entirety. Its the kind of place where good always prevails over evil, laughter and memories can be shared with the closest of friends, and any form of injustice that attempted to enter its gates would be swiftly dealt with. It's the kind of place where delicious food is just around the corner, where the innocence of children leads the way of discovery for adults; a place where it seems anything is possible.

Do you yearn for *that* kind of a place to reign in every corner of the world? Do you long for the peace and hope that you feel within the gates of the Magic Kingdom to be present in Chicago, San Diego, Peru, Russia and the ends of the earth?

I'm not talking about getting Imagineers to start a one world government so that everything has a Disney logo stamped on it. I'm talking about something deeper—the depth of what we yearn for becoming reality, the joy and peace becoming truly evident throughout the globe.

While some might scoff and say it's a pipe dream, I'm not alone in this hope. Throughout the Hebrew Scriptures, the ancient prophets dreamed of a day where calm would reign in the streets and there would be no more need for weapons because evil had ceased to exist. Take a moment to pause and envision this perfect place with the prophets:

> They will beat their swords into plowshares and their spears into pruning hooks. Nation will not take up sword against nation, nor will they train for war anymore.
> —Isaiah 2:4

> Once again men and women of ripe old age will sit in the streets of Jerusalem, each with cane in hand because of his age. The city streets will be filled with boys and girls playing there.
> —Zechariah 8:4-5

> The wolf will lie down with the lamb, the leopard will lie down with the goat, the calf and the lion and the yearling together; and a little child will lead them. The infant will play near the hole of the cobra, and the young child put his hand into the viper's nest.
> —Isaiah 11:6,8

That last verse from the prophet Isaiah seems especially troubling, considering it's talking about little babies sticking their tiny hands down into the holes of large venomous snakes...but that's only because we're thinking through the lens of our modern, danger-laden world.

Can you imagine the kind of place where you no longer had to worry about *anything*, from poisonous creatures to power hungry warlords; from pandemics to natural disasters? This is exactly the kind of planet that the prophets dare to dream would one day become reality, a time where God would make all things new. The apostle Peter thought back to the imagination of these prophets as he spoke to a crowd about the plan of Jesus after his resurrection and ascension:

> He must remain in heaven until the time comes for God to restore everything, as he promised long ago through his holy prophets.
> —Acts 3:21

He will restore and heal the rift that racism has caused in our world?

Everything.

What about the hunger pangs of children who do not have enough to eat, or the cracked and dried lips of those in communities without clean water to drink?

Everything.

Will He even restore the brokenness of creation itself, ending the devastation of typhoons, tornadoes, and earthquakes?

Everything.

At the end of the Bible, there's a book called Revelation that gives yet another picture of this new world, what it refers to as "the new Jerusalem":

> Now the dwelling of God is with men, and he will live with them. They will be his people, and God himself will be with them and be their God. He will wipe away every tear from their eyes. There will be no more death or mourning or crying or pain, for the old order of things has passed away.
> —Revelation 21:3-4

A few moments later in the same passage, Jesus is recorded as saying that "these words are trustworthy and true." We can be sure that all of the things that cause us grief will not exist anymore, from the natural disasters to the pain humans inflict on each other—but it won't end with those things alone being restored and redeemed.

See, it's not enough for me to stop at envisioning a world where violence and tragedies cease. Maybe I'm being a little greedy, but there's still a missing puzzle piece in the image of that envisioned perfect world that we've presented thus far: the people who I have loved and lost over the years I've spent in this life.

When I yearn to get back to Walt Disney World, it's not just because I want to check out Galaxy's Edge or to experience one of my favorite older attractions. Even more than those things, I am drawn to the kind of memories that being on property always seem to create with the people I love the most. Among my favorite are those with my brother Nick in childhood, a weekend at Night of Joy with my cousin Jake and friend Seth, and yet another trip with two of my best friends Emilee and Matt where they experienced Disney for the first time.

When I talk about the hope of an eternal life spent with those I love, I'm not just talking about those who have died like my brother or my grandparents. There are so many more individuals I have met and loved over the years who, for various reasons, I no longer can see very often (or at all).

If that promised place is coming, that "new Jerusalem" that some simply call Heaven, then I need it to include the possibility for those I love to be there as well. If I can take part in a place where there is no longer any pain or sadness *and* be reunited with those I love to make even greater memories than ever before...then *that* is truly a perfect place.

Those who know me best know that I am often very uninterested in long and heated debates about Heaven. There are so many cheesy paintings of Heaven, which makes it look like a place of clouds and bright lights, where people sit around with stupid smiles on their faces. I don't get how you're smiling that big when apparently all there is to do is play a harp on a fluffy cloud.

It's not that I am against the idea of Heaven or that I do not believe in it, but instead I would much rather talk about becoming a part of the Kingdom of Heaven in this life (like we did in chapter 10), because it's something I can take part in right now, right here, today.

In the midst of all of that, though, I recently listened to an old song from the band Relient K, an original from their Christmas album. When I finished the song, I was filled with hope for a life after this life.

In that place, there is no need to say goodbye. Relient K paints a picture of this reality, a Christmas where somehow all of the people he loves the most are present, singing in one voice:

> It's finally Christmas and I'm home—I head indoors to get
> out of this weather... and I don't know how, but the closest
> friends I've ever had are all inside, singing together: "Merry
> Christmas, here's to many more."

And so in this place, my brother Nick is present with the rest of my family, alongside my dear friends who moved several hours away years ago, as well as those I love from my three trips to Cuba who it's hard to contact—and uncountable others like my neighbor Ron and my friend Rick's nephew Evan.

In the midst of that place, they're all singing together, laughing together, and telling stories together. There are introductions and meals and a growing sense of community that is unparalleled.

Is it even possible to paint something like that? Even a watercolor painting of this kind of community made by a six year old would be more hope filled than the professional ones that show everyone smiling in the clouds, because now we're talking about a new kind of life beginning.

A kind of life where goodbyes would not be necessary and devastation could not irreversibly change our future. While it might not be possible to paint, this ultimate hope of restoration is exactly what the Scriptures tells us are possible through Heaven in Christ.

At the end of the day, Walt Disney World is a signpost, a mirror, a reflection. While we all know there's no real magic or pixie dust, the parks allow us a tiny taste of a greater reality that we all long after—true community that is unbreakable in a safe and peaceful place where love gets the final word.

The Scriptures teach that this eternally hopeful life is available to us, and thankfully we don't need to save up our money to buy tickets to get through the gates. Some people have gotten a bit stressed over the years, thinking that maybe we have to do a bunch of good stuff to take part. But the best news about Heaven is summarized by an apostle named Paul:

> It is by grace you have been saved, through faith—and this is not of yourselves, it is the gift of God—not by works, so that no one can boast.
> —Ephesians 2:8-9

What do we need to do in order to experience this kind of true, unending community? According to Paul, it's not about doing good works. Instead, its just simple faith—placing our trust in the work of Christ on the cross and believing that He is Lord. That doesn't mean you can just say some "magic words" of a prayer and then do whatever evil you want—that's obviously not true belief.

As Uncle Ben said *way* too many times across the Spider-Man movies, "With great power comes great responsibility." The power to conquer death and be resurrected to Heaven will result in the responsibility to live a live submitted to Christ and his way, just like any other apprenticeship.

In light of the future hope of Heaven, our job is to live our lives right now with that final finish line always in mind. Whatever quests and adventures you might take up during this life, never lose sight of that concluding climactic scene. If you do, you'll fall right in line with the words of John to all apprentices of Jesus:

> And now, dear children, continue in him, so that when he appears we may be confident and unashamed before him at his coming.
> —1 John 2:28

I hope to see each and every one of you reading these words—not just in the Disney Parks to catch a ride on Test Track, but more importantly in the community of Heaven where we can share all the stories of our adventures.

And who knows? There might even be Mickey bars.

Who Tells Your Story

I'm not a hundred percent sure, but I think we can safely call *Hamilton* a Disney thing now. I mean, they added the animated Cinderella Castle intro montage to the beginning of the film for some reason, so doesn't that automatically make it officially a Disney thing?

When the musical was released on Disney+ on July 3, 2020, countless Disney fans fell in love with the music, the cast, and the inspiring message that haunts both acts. There's a continual theme of legacy:

> What is a legacy? It's planting seeds in a garden you never get to see. I wrote some notes at the beginning of a song someone will sing for me...

The question that continues to surface throughout the show is one of a legacy, not only for the characters like Aaron Burr and Eliza Hamilton but for the viewer. At the end of your life, will you have lived a life worth talking about? What will your legacy be?

One of the most important lines is sung by George Washington, and it's the part of the advice I want to leave you all with as we close out this book:

> Let me tell you what I wish I'd known when I was young and dreamed of glory—you have no control who lives, who dies, who tells your story.

Make no mistake, you are going to face those who oppose your God-given adventure. Some people will scoff, while others might tell you that you're making a mistake or being foolish because you're willing to attempt what seems impossible.

When facing that kind of negativity, it's important to remember two related things.

Firstly, that you will always have people who disagree with what you say or do, whether it's the right or wrong choice. Since people are going to complain either way, why not jump wholeheartedly into doing the right thing? All that truly matters is that you are following the call God has put on your life.

Secondly, you have no control over who tells your story. Your goal cannot be to get the highest accolades, awards, and compliments. The truth is, you might actually receive the opposite, like all those times Walt's hard work was referred to as a "folly." Regardless of how you're received, keep doing the right thing.

If you've gotten to the end of this book, you've now read over a hundred pages about living a meaningful legacy with your life. If you've been waiting for an official invitation or benediction to actually get started with some sort of action, I leave you with the words of—who else—Walter Elias Disney:

> The way to get started is to quit talking and begin doing.

Connect with Josh

It's an honor that you have decided to stay with me throughout this book. Over the next few years, I hope to continue to deepen this conversation through additional books, a related podcast, and my social media feeds.

If you're interested, you can find my podcast by subscribing to "Beyond the Pixie Dust" on your podcast player of choice. We'll be recording all of the episodes in surround sound right within various places all throughout Walt Disney World property, and I'll be joined for meaningful discussions on life with people like my friend Rick.

Additionally, feel free to follow me on Twitter @ beyonddust or via my Facebook page, facebook.com/ BeyondthePixieDust. I'll announce any further books that I may write into the future there, as well as on my website, www.beyondthepixiedust.com.

I also want to know more about you. I would love to hear more about your own journey, your personal adventure, or even a hint on where you think the best food is hiding at Walt Disney World.

We've spent a really long time together in the midst of these last pages, and I've just realized I don't even know your name.

Feel free to email me at beyondpixiedustpodcast@ gmail.com or give me a call at 234-759-9042.

Raise a glass to freedom...

Acknowledgments

To my best friend Carissa: Thank you for "forcing me" to write this book and for always encouraging me to follow my dreams. You are responsible for so many of my visions coming to fruition with your continued support. Thanks for tolerating my Disney obsession and never asking why I'm ordering yet *another* book on Walt Disney World. Best of wives and best of women...

Ellie: Right now, you're a little too young to fully understand what it means that I've completed a book involving WDW...but since you're just as obsessed with Disney as me, I can almost guarantee you're going to love this book someday. Thanks for being such a great friend in addition to being my daughter. I love you!

Eliza: As I write this, you are still a few months from being born. We can't wait to meet you and, obviously, I can't wait to begin introducing all sorts of Disney to another little person who gets to experience it all for the very first time. You will come of age with our young nation...

My friend Rick: Thanks for giving me the permission to share your story in this book. You continue to inspire me throughout the years, not only in physical running but also in running this race of life. (If any readers want to read more from him, you can check out his blog at http://runningwithrb.blogspot.com. You will not be disappointed in reading about the vast amounts of insane running adventures he decides to jump into.)

My brother in law Jay: Our many conversations about story and characters helped to influence this book, especially the chapter on Guides. Thanks for your role as a Guide in the lives of many around you, including mine.

My editor Bob McLain and his publishing empire Theme Park Press: It is because of you that these words are able to be held in the hands of the readers. You do massively important work, and I am so thankful for your role in making this dream of mine come true.

ABOUT THEME PARK PRESS

Theme Park Press publishes books primarily about the Disney company, its history, culture, films, animation, and theme parks, as well as theme parks in general.

Our authors include noted historians, animators, Imagineers, and experts in the theme park industry.

We also publish many books by first-time authors, with topics ranging from fiction to theme park guides.

And we're always looking for new talent. If you'd like to write for us, or if you're interested in the many other titles in our catalog, please visit:

www.ThemeParkPress.com

• •

Theme Park Press Newsletter

Subscribe to our free email newsletter and enjoy:

- ◆ Free book downloads and giveaways
- ◆ Access to excerpts from our many books
- ◆ Announcements of forthcoming releases
- ◆ Exclusive additional content and chapters
- ◆ And more good stuff available nowhere else

To subscribe, visit www.ThemeParkPress.com, or send email to newsletter@themeparkpress.com.

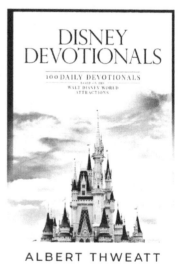

Read more about these books
and our many other titles at:

www.ThemeParkPress.com